silence

silence

Christina Feldman

RODALE

© 2001 Axis Publishing

Conceived and created by
Axis Publishing Limited
8c Accommodation Road
London NW11 8ED
www.axispublishing.co.uk

Published in North America in 2001 by
Rodale, Inc.
33 E. Minor Street
Emmaus, PA 18098
www.rodale.com

This edition printed 2001

Axis Publishing
Designer: Siân Keogh
Editor: Matthew Harvey

Rodale Organic Living Books
Executive Editor: Kathleen DeVanna Fish
Art Director: Patricia Field
Project Manager: Christine Bucks

Library of Congress Catalog No. 2001003328
ISBN 0-87596-937-2 (alk. paper)

Printed and bound by Star Standard, Singapore

Distributed in the book trade by St. Martin's Press

2 4 6 8 10 9 7 5 3 1 hardcover

 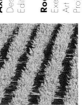  

RODALE

WE INSPIRE AND ENABLE PEOPLE TO IMPROVE
THEIR LIVES AND THE WORLD AROUND THEM

contents

introduction

As we emerge from the haste and clamor of the world, glimpses of silence startle us into a new wakefulness and sense of wonder. We awaken on a winter morning to the stillness of a world lying hushed beneath a blanket of overnight snow. Silence permeates the church in the moments before the service begins; the restlessness and chatter die away to be replaced by a collective calmness and sense of reverence. The chimes of the monastery bell are heard in a silent meditation room, greeted as a call to awareness. We walk into the welcome silence of our home after a day filled with sound and busyness, and feel soothed by its presence. Walking through the powerful silence of a forest, we are embraced in its stillness and learn to listen, see, and feel more deeply.

The moments of silence we encounter are benedictions, blessings that echo in our hearts. They invite us to be still, to listen deeply, and to be present in this world. The glimpses of silence we encounter in the world are potent intimations of the inner stillness possible for each of us. The glimpses of silence we meet remind us of a way of being in which we are deeply touched by the mystery and grandeur of life. In the midst of silence we remember what it feels like to be truly alive, receptive, and sensitive. Silence, we come to understand, is the language of the heart.

Silence is a treasure that is becoming increasingly elusive. We are the most affluent, successful, **powerful** of all generations. We are also the busiest and perhaps the noisiest. On a cellular level we intuitively know the richness and value of silence, yet we sadly neglect its cultivation. Bombarded by sound, information, and sensory input, we feel the effects in our hearts and bodies of being exiled from silence. We thirst for meaning, freedom, **inner** spaciousness, and peace, yet too often forget that silence is the medium for their discovery. We need silence to listen to our own heart and to touch the heart of another. The Chinese sage Lao-tzu, who lived and taught in the sixth century, reminds us: "Take time to listen to what is said without words, to obey the law too subtle to be written, to **worship** the unnameable and to embrace the unformed."

Silence lies at the heart of all the great **spiritual** traditions. Through it we can dive beneath words, ideas, chatter, and concepts to discover the unspoken truths and the unfathomable mystery of **being**. The variety of forms of contemplation, prayer, and meditation meet in their reverence for silence. Through them we learn to still the clamor of our hearts and the competing voices that cascade through our mind and to discover a place of profound stillness and receptivity. Silence is not a vacuum or a barren desert of the heart, but the source of **creativity**, love, compassion, and transforming wisdom.

Spiritual traditions embrace silence as a beloved friend, cultivate it, celebrate it, and probe its potential. In the presence of the sacred we naturally descend into silence. At the Wailing Wall in Jerusalem, the Bodhi Tree in Bodhgaya, the Black Stone in Mecca, or on the banks of the River Ganges in India there is a tangible silence that has little to do with the absence of sound. These are dedicated places that remind us of the ancient quest for peace, wisdom, and stillness. We are reminded that greatness of heart is not just the territory of the saints and the sages of the past, but a possibility to be realized in our own life. When the Dalai Lama, the exiled leader of Tibet, speaks, his words invariably fall into a well of deep silence. His unswerving message is to remember our place in this world, the goodness in our own hearts, our undeniable relationship with one another, and to find ways to live with the greatest integrity, compassion, and peace.

Silence is a way of bearing witness to truth. In the silent

revolution in Czechoslovakia, hundreds of thousands of people gathered together, a silent testimony to freedom. The candle flames held in their hands spoke more than a thousand words. Silent marches of protest against racism, oppression, violence, and torture call us to listen, to understand, and to be a witness to pain and the need for transformation. During the Civil Rights Movement, thousands of black students would walk silently through jeering, threatening crowds. It was a silence of profound dignity and truth that changed people's hearts and ultimately changed their world.

In the face of tragedy and sorrow, silence is at times the only gift of the heart we feel able to offer. In the aftermath of the 1995 Oklahoma city bombing tragedy, in which 168 people, including 19 children, were killed in a few moments of terrible destruction, the world was stunned into silence. There were no words to convey the empathy, compassion, and sorrow that echoed in our hearts. There were no explanations that could ease the grief and pain of the bereaved families and friends. Sitting at the bedside of a beloved in the last days of their life, words communicate less than the intimacy of a loving silence. There are times when we need to stand together in silence, be together in silence, and accompany each other in this life in silence. In those moments we meet in the depths of our being and see ourselves reflected in the heart of another. The intimacy of silence reminds us that we are never truly alone.

Silence asks us to see our lives and the world we live in with fresh eyes, to look at things from a different angle. It asks us to question all of our previous assumptions about ourselves and the way we live, replacing complacency, habit, and prejudice with a willingness to be fully present and alert to the lessons of each moment. Silence asks us to find the peace and meaning that are present at the center of our lives—no matter how busy our schedule may be. We assume a receptive attitude in silence which is not passive, submissive, or lazy. As we set out on the path to explore silence, we open our hearts and minds to the insights and lessons that await us.

In Washington, a length of black, polished stone carries the names of those who died in the war in Vietnam. The war is long over; the protests, violence, arguments, and hatred that so permeated that time have been replaced by new cycles of argument and dissent. People visit in silence, sometimes to lay a flower, to weep, or just to touch an inscribed name. The wall is a symbol of human catastrophe, conflict, and loss. Its silent presence asks us to remember what it is we truly value, what gives meaning, what heals us, and the need to end the wars in our hearts.

Great joy, as well as great sorrow, takes us into a realm of appreciation and celebration that words cannot describe. If we stand in front of a stunning sculpture, walk through a pristine wilderness, be present at the birth of a child, our hearts burst with the wonder of life. Silence is our way of paying homage, of bowing to the moment. In the moments before the words come, we sense a profound inner stillness and richness of being. We are truly alive in the presence of a remarkable life. Within that silence we glimpse an experience of oneness and communion in which all divisions fall away. The poetry of enlightenment celebrates this joy in simple words that convey the depth of happiness and freedom that awaits our discovery. A Japanese Zen master, Basho, writes

Speechless before

These budding green

Spring leaves

In blazing sunlight.

Silence is a teacher; within it we learn some of the deepest lessons of our lives about aloneness and intimacy, joy and sorrow, conflict and peace. When we speak less to the world and everything in it, we bring a silence in which we can listen to the story of life, other people, and our own heart. We learn to treasure listening and the richness it offers more than the busyness of our conclusions, assumptions, knowledge, or opinions. We are humbled by silence as we discover that our words can never fully describe the fullness and richness of any moment in our life that is truly listened to. There is so much we don't know, so much that cannot be explained, and we learn to embrace and welcome that mystery. Taking nothing for granted, we enter each moment like a visitor, willing to see anew and to be touched by each unfolding moment. We discover within ourselves the willingness to be surprised and understand that our potential to deepen as a human being relies upon our capacity to be surprised. We learn the joy of the present.

Silence is a refuge. There are times in our life when our worlds fall apart, when we are overwhelmed by the intensity of events, when we feel alienated from ourselves or others, and when our life seems to make no sense. In those moments when we feel most adrift and confused, silence offers a sanctuary of renewal. In moments of confusion and complexity we are tempted to do more, to act, to find explanations, to speak. If we listen to our heart, we come to know the wisdom of being still. We calm the turmoil of our mind, feeling our feet on the earth, and connecting once more with a depth of inner silence that can guide us, heal us, and restore us.

In moments of heartfelt connection and intimacy, silence is a shared room of peace and ease. Close friends and partners find a way of being together in silence that is respectful, sensitive, and trusting. It is a silence that communicates a deep love and care that no longer require the reassurance of words. It is a silence of unconditional acceptance and warmth.

Silence, in its most authentic meaning, is vast, spacious, calm, and peaceful. Sadly, silence is also used as an instrument of abuse and punishment. In conflicted families silence embodies a withholding of love and affection; it is used to isolate, reject, and punish. Those who have experienced this misuse of silence carry its memory through their life and tend to interpret all silence as dangerous and threatening.

Countless people in our world are made invisible and powerless through the silence enforced upon them. The elderly, the oppressed, homosexuals, women, children, and dissidents are cast into the shadows of life through the gagging of their voice. In a military prison lives a man sentenced to solitary confinement for murdering a prison guard. Enforced upon him is the order for "no human contact." For years he hasn't heard the voice of another human being, he hasn't spoken, hasn't been touched. In truth he is a walking dead man. Silence, misused, is a weapon of isolation and a form of torture. The abandoned heart is disenfranchised from life and love.

Just as misused silence damages, wise silence heals. Too many communities, families, and relationships in our world are scarred by conflict, struggle, anger, and division. We argue with one another, judge and condemn, hurl insults, and lose ourselves in trying to shout louder than our opponent. Silence teaches us to listen to our enemies and adversaries. What difference would it make to join our worst enemy in a few moments of silence? In silence we open to the simple reality that just as we yearn for happiness, acceptance, understanding, and compassion, so do our enemies. Just as we have the capacity to experience pain, grief, loneliness, and fear, so do they. Where do hatred, division, and conflict end but in those precious moments of silence that bring depth and the possibility of a new beginning?

All of us in our life

encounter moments of profound silence. The clamor and discordant voices still, and we are faced with a stillness that is rich in potential. Silence can seem like an accident, an unexpected and unpredictable encounter. Learning to heed those moments of silence, we perhaps begin to understand that silence is not an accident, but an ever-present reality revealed to us in the moments when we remember to listen. Silence is revealed in moments of wholehearted attention, when we are fully present in this life. A Christian mystic reminds us, "Absolute, unmixed attention is prayer." The art of cultivating silence does not take us to a destination divorced from the present moment of reality in our life. Cultivating the art of silence, we learn to discover its richness in all moments and encounters. Treasuring its rich potential, we learn to discover what it means to live with a silent heart, rich in vitality, creativity, energy, and life.

In the Bhagavad Gita, one of the sacred texts of the East, it is said

"Teach us that even as the wonder of the stars in the heavens only reveals itself in the silence of the night, so the wonder of life reveals itself in the silence of the heart. In the silence of our heart we may see the scattered leaves of all the universe bound by love."

Silence is the ground of happiness, communion, and oneness.

We can learn to find it in all moments and things; we discover it has never been lost but is only hidden.

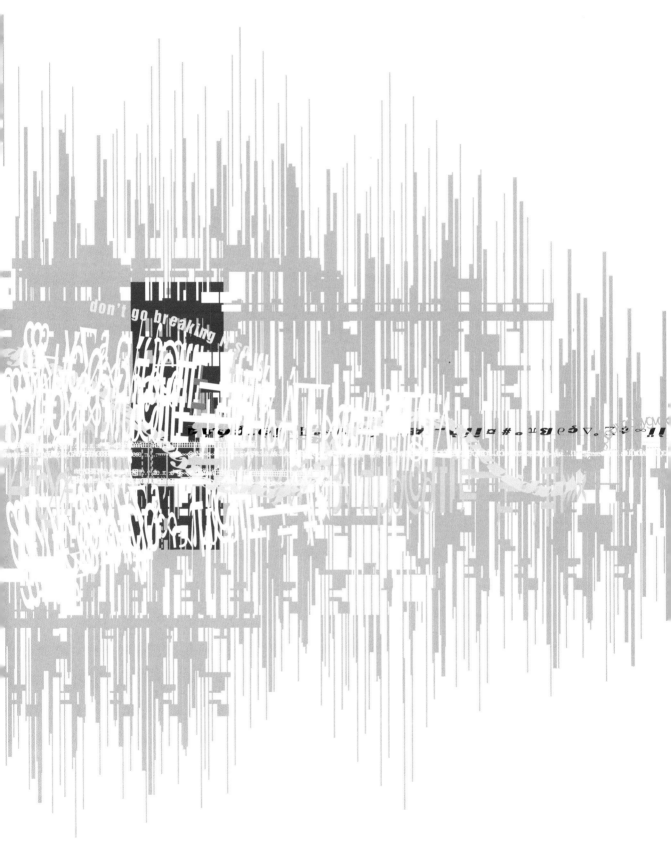

don't go breaking

1

In silence we meet **ourselves**

In silence we embrace the **universe**

Tibetan monks and nuns continue to enclose themselves in small caves, the entrances bricked over, for months and years, to heed the inner call of freedom. Within those enclosed, silent spaces they contemplate and learn to listen deeply to the rhythm of life.

There is a time for letting the words fall away, to retreat into one's own heart and to meet the beauty of the moment with receptive stillness. It is a time of inner enclosure and of creating a sacred space.

A HISTORY OF SILENCE

love can be found within our own hearts

The journey into silence lies at the heart of all great spiritual traditions. The ancient stories of the sages and mystics speak to us of the pilgrimage into silence and the richness it reveals. In the past and in the present, silence is embraced as the root of revelation, of oneness, of transformation and mystical experience. The timeless stories of silence and transformation inspire us and guide us to travel in our own hearts beyond the limits of individual experience. They are stories of possibility, that teach us not to despair or be lost in hopelessness but to look anew at our own stories and lives. They teach us to discover the silence within our hearts where great courage, compassion, and love can be found.

In the early Christian tradition women and men left behind them the turbulence of the marketplace to make their home in the silence of the desert. Renouncing the world of busyness, activity, and engagement they settled in the austerity of the desert, embracing its stillness and simplicity. Families, friends, companionship, reassurance, and comfort were forsaken to seek a deeper richness in solitude and silence. Just as Jesus spent forty days in the silence of the desert before beginning his teaching, the early Desert Fathers and Mothers embraced stillness so they could listen to the same voice that guided Christ. Mother Teresa, the European nun who felt called to care for the sick and the dying in Calcutta, reminds us, "God cannot be found in noise and restlessness. God is the friend of silence."

Silence empowers us. Stilling the clutter and clamor of our minds and life, we find the focus and clarity needed to end pain, alienation, oppression, and fear.

Daily life in many cloistered monasteries continues to honor the Grand Silence. There is a time for letting the words fall away, to retreat into one's own heart, and to meet the beauty of the moment with receptive stillness. It is a time of inner enclosure and of creating a sacred space. The Grand Silence is never seen as a punishment but as pregnant with potential. It is the garden of contemplation and spiritual depth. In her writings, Teresa of Avila, one of the great Christian mystics, invites us to imagine that there is within us a palace of great richness with many rooms to explore. Within this inner palace we discover something incomparably deeper and more precious than anything outside ourselves. Silence teaches us that we are far from barren or empty inside, but that through stillness we will discover a world mysterious, rich, and indescribable.

In the early Buddhist traditions, long before the establishment of Buddhist monasteries and hundreds of years before the birth of Jesus Christ, monks and nuns

Their stories reflect a universal, timeless wisdom, a depth of compassion and integrity and a celebration of silence. The joy and peace etched upon their faces tells its own story.

the inner call of freedom

would go into the jungles and caves and up to the mountaintops seeking seclusion and silence. Heeding the central teachings of the Buddha, that true freedom would be discovered only within our own hearts, they disengaged from the world in order to fully embrace solitude. Tibetan monks and nuns continue to pursue this experience of solitude, enclosing themselves in small caves, the entrances bricked over, for months and years, to heed the inner call of freedom. Within those enclosed, silent spaces they contemplate, **meditate**, and learn to listen deeply to the rhythm of life. From the deserts, mountaintops, and caves these women and men have returned to the world to teach, to engage and tell their stories. These stories reflect a universal, timeless wisdom, a depth of compassion and integrity, and a celebration of silence. The joy and peace etched upon their faces tells its own story.

This profound inner journey is succinctly told in the stories and poems of the ox herder in the Zen tradition of Buddhism. The ox herder's journey begins in darkness and confusion as he faces a maze of countless crisscrossing paths. He knows that he is seeking the elusive ox, **enlightenment**, but is afraid and uncertain of what path to follow. His journey takes him farther and farther from the settled lands of his

Faith in silence is the sign of perfect equilibrium.

Silence is the absolute poise or balance of body, mind and spirit.

As we listen to the stories of the mystics and sages who have embraced silence as a beloved, we learn that silence is not passive.

home into unfamiliar, frightening territory, yet he has no choice but to go on. On his journey he faces many perils as he searches for the elusive ox. He is alone and must reach deep within himself to find the strength and courage to continue. Discovering the ox, he must learn how to befriend it, be intimate with it, and listen to it before it will take him to the peace of the mountaintop. There he discovers freedom, vastness, and the compassion that takes him back to the marketplace. Unconventional in his manner and dress, his face wreathed in smiles, he reenters the world, and all gates open before him.

In the tribal traditions of the Native American, silence is honored as the home of renewal and of communion with the natural world. Moments of silence are sought as the place where our natural role in the universe is affirmed. The sun, the trees, the moon, the rivers, and the wind are all honored in the process, thus reminding individuals of their essential interdependence and connection with this world. The elders of the tribes speak of their profound faith in silence as the sign of perfect equilibrium. Silence, they say, "is the absolute poise or balance of body, mind and spirit. At ease in silence, the warrior stands firm and unshaken by the storms of life. If you ask him what silence is, he will answer 'It is the Great Mystery.'"

The silence of the initiation is embraced as the home of renewal and regeneration, the womb of wisdom.

In the Navajo tradition, silence lies at the hearts of the initiations and rituals that mark significant life transitions. To honor the turning of a boy into a man, a girl into a woman—and a child into an adult—the familiar journey of seclusion in silence, transformation, and emergence is undertaken. The young boy or girl leaves their home and family, encouraged and honored by the entire village. They create a sacred space in seclusion and enter into an inner journey. It is a time for inner listening, attuning themselves to their interior landscape and finding self-reliance and inner authority. They are saying farewell to the world of their childhood and giving birth to themselves as an adult and respected member of their community. In their solitude they learn to find the inner resources of courage, trust, and steadfastness that sustain them. Emerging, they are greeted by their community as a person of dignity and fearlessness, honored as a contributing, respected equal possessing a voice of wisdom. The silence of the initiation is embraced as the home of renewal and regeneration, the womb of wisdom.

The cultivation of silence continues to lie at the heart of spiritual traditions. Everywhere in the world pilgrims and **seekers** continue to create and foster spaces of silence in which the still, clear voice of the sacred can be heard. In the Jewish tradition, as the Sabbath nears, the daily tasks and activities are put aside, the work of the world is laid down, and stillness descends. It is a time to attend to the spirit, to celebrate the mystery of creation.

Somewhere in this world at this moment, there is a man or woman secluded in a cave, shivering on a mountaintop, or enclosed in a monastic cell. They may be invisible to us as they follow this age-old tradition, yet they are the spiritual mothers and fathers who will continue to remind us of our own potential to find freedom, vastness, and the presence of the sacred in each of us. Their chosen pilgrimage may seem alien, impossible, or even repugnant to us, yet they give life to the tradition of silence and continue to be a powerful **symbol** of the sacred that lingers long in our hearts.

We have all had glimpses of the benediction of silence and are reminded through them of what truly matters in our lives. Moments of deep silence and the openings they evoke are not strangers to any of us. We glimpse the power of silence walking in the forest, when the chatter of our minds stills and we experience a deep sensitivity and harmony. Silence can express itself in a variety of rich experiences. It is the welcome warmth of shared **intimacy** with a close friend, when our judgments and assumptions fall away and we know a deep communion. We are taken by surprise when, in a moment alone, the clamor of our thoughts ceases, our need for busyness calms, and we find ourselves present in this universe in a way that speaks to us of our wholeness and the abundance of stillness. In all those moments we glimpse the rich spiritual seam of silence and are invited to explore its possibilities. The heartfelt connection with this life that we long for and search for is found in the pilgrimage each one of us makes into silence.

silence
empowers

As we listen to the stories of the mystics and sages who have embraced silence as a beloved, we learn that silence is not passive, alienated, or lifeless. Within its depths is found an abundance of energy, creativity, love, and wisdom. The sages do not return from the deserts and mountaintops dysfunctional, depressed, or indifferent, but with a profound patience, tolerance, and commitment to transformation. Silence, it seems, is not a surrender of personal freedom. It is the place where we connect with our deepest values and discover freedom within our own heart. Silence is not even the opposite of speech, but a way to find the truths that need to be spoken and a way of speaking them so that they can be heard.

Silence, we come to understand, is not a denial of life, love, or community, but teaches us to celebrate the beauty of each moment. Silence empowers us. Stilling the chatter and clamor of our minds and our worries about life, we find the focus and clarity needed to end pain, alienation, oppression, and fear.

Throughout his life, Mahatma Gandhi affirmed the unshakable power and creativity of silence. The tradition of nonviolent protest and transformation has its roots in silence. In seeking the freedom of his country and people, Gandhi soon realized the futility of endless argument or reasoning. During his many periods of imprisonment Gandhi would undertake a voluntary silence as a necessary space for reflection, renewal, and regeneration. Through silence he formulated the pathway of "satyagraha," the movement that has come to be known as "soul force" or "truth force." He went on to teach that many people could resist words but few people could resist the power of silent truth.

Gandhi counseled all his followers to adopt periods of voluntary silence and to find the power and fearlessness within it that would be needed to overturn the might of the occupying British army with all its

As we listen to the stories of the mystics and sages who have embraced silence as a beloved, we learn that silence is not passive, alienated, or lifeless. Within its depths is found an abundance of energy, creativity, love, and wisdom.

Gandhi taught his followers that if you were not to be overcome by the forces of anger and hatred surrounding you, you would need to discover the inner equilibrium that could embrace the inner rage and violence. This powerful model of nonviolent, silent protest continues to transform oppression in our world. In silence we meet ourselves; in silence we befriend ourselves; in silence we embrace the universe. Through silence we learn to act and speak with true wisdom, courage, and compassion.

The tradition of nonviolent protest and transformation has its roots in silence

forces. To meet an armed force knowing you were about to be beaten, wounded, hurt, or even killed, required a kind of inner balance and courage that would be found only through having embraced one's own inner forces of fear, anger, and hatred. Gandhi taught his followers that if you were not to be overcome by the apparently unmovable forces of anger and hatred surrounding you, you would need to discover the inner equilibrium that could embrace the inner rage and violence. This inspiring model of nonviolent, silent power has established a tradition of peaceful protest that continues to transform oppression in our world. Through silence we learn to act and speak with true wisdom, courage, and compassion.

We can all draw upon the wisdom in the timeless traditions of seclusion, transformation, and emergence. Our own spiritual pilgrimage will not be the replica of anyone else's journey. Yet we see our own story reflected in the story of every single person who has set out on a journey to find the depths of freedom and compassion.

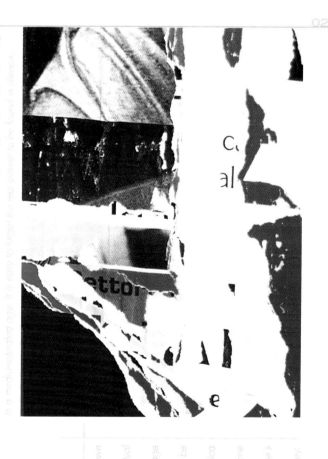

stand

back

from

busyness

lives and hearts of ordinary people

Profound stillness is not just the territory of the ancient mystics and sages. The power of transformation and the richness of spiritual illumination are not the domain of a saintly or spiritually gifted elect.

tossed by the storms of existence

journey

into

silence

029

In our yearning for stillness and communion, we know the need to calm the chaos and turbulence of our inner and outer worlds. Experiencing what it means to be tossed by the storms of existence, we know the need to discover a refuge of stillness in our own heart. Riding the perpetual roller coaster of our thoughts, anxieties, and hopes, we long to discover a profound stillness and poise. No one can substitute for us in this journey, no matter how wise or loving; no one can deliver silence to us. We ourselves must learn how to listen, to dive beneath the waves of restlessness and discover the heart of silence.

There are times when each of us needs to stand back from the busyness of our lives, to seclude ourselves and turn our attention within. We may not be drawn to the cloisters of a monastic cell or to a mountain cave, but we are all drawn to the peace and richness found in silence. In the midst of our lives, we can learn the art of creating sacred spaces, times of listening,

and moments of pause. Within these spaces we listen to the truths and gifts of each present moment that bloom in stillness. These spaces of stillness are the places where we rediscover ourselves, renew ourselves, and find the balance and wisdom to reenter our life with a heart filled with compassion and balance.

Profound stillness is not just the territory of the ancient mystics and sages. The power of transformation and the richness of spiritual illumination are not the domain of a saintly, or spiritually gifted elect. Listening to stories of illumination, we are invited into the lives and hearts of ordinary people with an extraordinary dedication to love, oneness, and depth. Silence is here in our life; silence is here in our heart—it beckons to us. Heeding its invitation, we discover profound psychological and spiritual realities and we understand that we are part of the lineage of silence that transcends all barriers of time and tradition. When we learn to be still, the history of silence comes alive in our present.

silence is the first **casualty**

sound is the voice of **life**

Thirsting for greater ease and silence in our life

and heart, we travel to distant places of the world,

believing that silence is a geographical place

rather than a dimension of consciousness.

Amid all the bustle, monks and nuns attend to their meditative practice; moving serenely through the crowds, raking the paths, and focusing intently upon each step they take.

WHAT IS NOISE?

seclusion is no guarantee of silence

Every year countless people travel to Asian monasteries, stressed, adrift, and desperately looking for a refuge from the storms of the world and the intensity of their lives. Contrary to their expectations, they are often appalled to discover that many Asian monasteries are

the **noisiest** places on earth. Transistor radios blare; every day seems to be a festival attended by bustling crowds of villagers; the stray dogs congregate, barking; traffic noise is incessant; and chanting is broadcast over loudspeakers. Amid all the bustle, monks and nuns attend to their meditative practice, moving serenely through the crowds, raking the paths, and focusing intently upon each step they take, each breath they breathe, and each discourse they listen to. They carry within them into each activity a **visible serenity** and stillness. New Western students can usually be found in the abbot's hut within days of their arrival, complaining that the bustle and noise of the monastery were the very experiences they were trying to **escape** from. Smiling, the abbot will generally answer, "What noise?"

as our technology

progresses the

range of our noise

spreads

Silence is what frees us to listen well, to live with

authenticity and discover wholeness within ourselves.

The stillness within the busy monastery challenges the view we hold that silence is the opposite of sound. Chuang-tzu, a Chinese Taoist master of the fourth century, taught that "the sage is not quiet because quietness is said to be good. He is quiet because the multitude of things cannot disturb his quietude. The mind of a sage is the mirror of heaven and earth in which all things are reflected."

Noise, it seems, infiltrates every area of our life, permeating every corner of our world. Our lives are often governed by chronic, continuous cycles of activity and busyness. Words fill our every waking hour; our desk calendars overflow with appointments, we rarely come to the end of the lists of tasks that remain to be done. Compelled by busyness, our minds spin faster and faster, and we rarely make an appointment with silence. As our technology progresses, the range of our noise spreads. It is increasingly difficult to find anywhere in our world that is a truly silent place. Even the silence of a remote Himalayan cave is likely to be **interrupted** by the ring of a passing trekker's cellphone. We live in a world becoming increasingly rich in its varied uses of sound, thought, and language, yet on a personal level, we may have surrendered the art and wisdom of silence.

On occasion, we find ourselves listening to the sound of silence. The air conditioning switches off; the hum of the refrigerator fades away; there is a pause in the sound of the traffic outside our window, and we **breathe** a sigh of relief. A mother who lived beneath an airport flight path recounted that she could see her children's shoulders

We find ourselves

listening to the

sound of silence.

Words fill our every working hour, our desk calendars overflow with appointments, we rarely come to the end of the list of tasks that remain to be done. Compelled by busyness, our minds spin faster and faster, and we rarely make an appointment with silence.

drop, releasing tension, when the background sound of planes' landings and takeoffs would pause. There are moments in all of our lives when silence beckons to us and awakens a memory of its richness. Stillness, we come to understand, is not a luxury or hobby, it is pivotal to our well-being. Silence is what frees us to listen well to ourselves and others, to live with authenticity and discover wholeness within ourselves.

None of us are strangers to the cumulative effects of too much busyness. The tension is stored in our bodies, we are prone to impatience, frustration, and rage, and our minds collapse under the pressure of cascading thoughts. Our hearts ache with sadness over all the moments we have neglected and the people and things we have left unattended. The sunset we missed, the friend fallen by the wayside, the partner we did not have time to care for, the child we were too busy to listen to. In the midst of the turbulence and demands of our days, we find ourselves longing for stillness, for peace, for silence.

Our tasks and activities are
seen to be so critical and
never-ending that our spirit
bows beneath the weight
of our life.

The incessant chatter of our own minds
creates a pressure greater than anything in the world.

We sense a growing urgency in our minds to "get away," to "find some space," or to change our lives. We are seeking peace, stillness, and a return to a gentler way of being in this life. We understand that there must be more to our life than speeding up its tempo. Thomas Merton, the 20th-century American mystic, wrote, "There is a pervasive form of contemporary violence that is overwork. The rush and pressure of modern life are a form, perhaps the most common form, of its innate violence. To allow oneself to be carried away by a multitude of conflicting concerns, to surrender to too many demands, to commit oneself to too many projects, to want to help everyone in everything, is to succumb to violence."

Silence is the first casualty of our addiction to busyness. We all want our lives to be valuable, to be helpful and productive, yet in our rush to accomplish, we rarely create the spaces to listen, to explore the gaps between events, and we find ourselves overwhelmed. Our

tasks and activities are seen to be so critical and never-ending that our spirit bows beneath the weight of our life. One of the outstanding dangers of busyness is that we smother the wisdom of silence, are deafened to authentic intuition, and can no longer appreciate the countless quiet moments that speak to us of peace, joy, and stillness. In Chinese calligraphy the word for "busy" is composed of two characters that are translated as "heart" and "killing."

Thirsting for greater ease and silence in our lives and hearts, we travel to distant corners of the world, believing that silence may be a geographical place, rather than a dimension of consciousness. Our search for silence grows in equal proportion to our feeling of being overwhelmed by sound and activity. We seal our windows, purchase earplugs, and try to close our door to the world, desperately searching for an exit from the babble of the world. We believe we have to divorce ourselves from the world to find silence, to cease interactions and become hermits. The degree to which we

The discordant voices that compete for attention, the judgments, plans, rehearsals of the future all stifle stillness within us. The endless replaying of our memories and daydreams suffocates silence. Our wish to flee from the noise of the world may be a disguised wish to flee from the noise of our own internal monologues.

to try to protect ourselves from the intrusion of life is the degree that stress increases and that we cease to experience our life directly. We create the dichotomy between sound and silence that leads us to a futile pursuit of silence as if it could be owned. We do not have to choose between silence and sound, stillness or activity. The polarization of them exists only in our own minds.

Our journey to peace and authenticity asks us to attend to the link and rhythm between sound and silence and to discover the harmony that already exists between the two. Wherever we go in this world, our minds accompany us. Seclusion is no guarantee of silence or peace. The shivering aspirant in his Himalayan cave ponders how to make the cicadas stop chirping or plans the wonderful book he will write of his experiences. Each one of us has an average of 67,000 thoughts a day, and most of them we have thought a thousand times before. Essentially, each one of us writes a major book in our mind each day of our life. The discordant voices that compete for attention, the judgments, plans, rehearsals of the future all stifle stillness within us. The endless replaying of our memories and daydreams suffocates silence. Our wish to flee from the noise of the world may be a disguised wish to flee from the noise of our own internal monologues. The incessant chatter of our own mind creates a pressure greater than anything in the world.

Each morning and evening, on a death row cellblock, several inmates reach beneath their bunks and pull out their meditation mats and cushions. From a background of different faiths, they come together in creating, for an hour, a sacred space. Sitting in silence, they are surrounded by the sounds of the prison—the crashing of the cell doors, shouted conversations and jeers, the radios and commands of the guards. The world doesn't stop for the quiet inmates, and the bars remain, yet they are learning to listen in a different way. In those hours together they learn how to reclaim stillness, peace, and serenity.

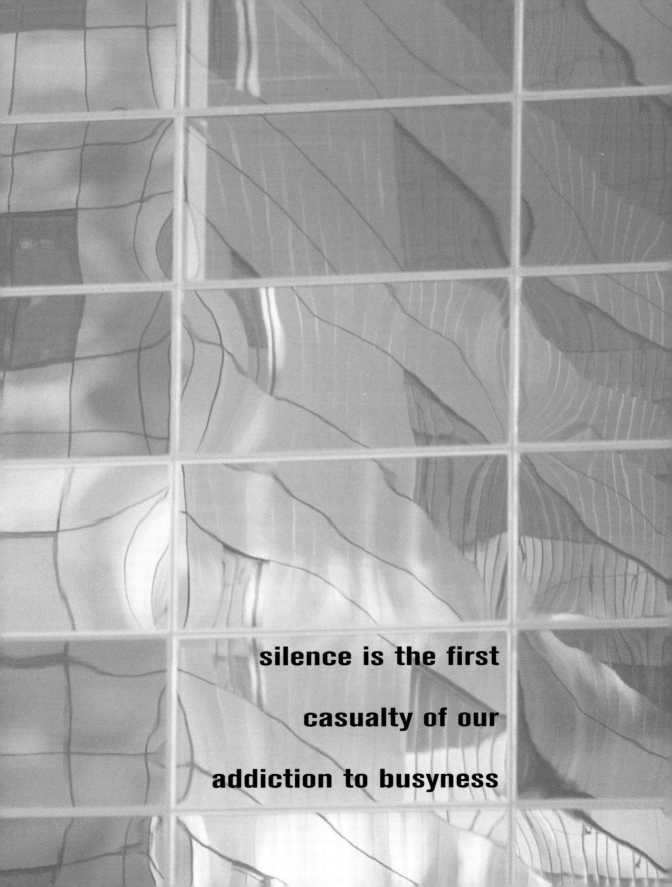

silence is the first

casualty of our

addiction to busyness

Noise is what happens

when we cannot listen. To an

attentive mother, a baby's cry

is a sound to be embraced.

To someone else it is just a

racket. Noise is what

Is there anywhere in this world where there is no sound? When we go to the mountaintop do we still need to listen to something? The sound of the wind stirring the branches of the trees and the raindrops bouncing off the leaves will be there. In a flotation tank you hear your heartbeat and the pulse of your blood circulating in your body. Sound is the voice of life. Composer John Cage remarked, "My favorite piece of music is the one we hear all the time if we are quiet." As long as we view silence as the opposite of sound we will always feel intruded upon and assaulted by life. What is the difference between noise and sound? Sounds are always happening around us and within us. Life continues to sing its song and to tell its story.

Noise is what happens when we cannot listen. To an attentive mother, a baby's cry is a sound to be embraced. To someone else it is just a racket. Alienated from inner stillness, we experience much of the sound in our world as an assault. We try to protect ourselves from incoming sounds, sheltering behind our fragile defenses and becoming increasingly stressed as the bombardment relentlessly continues. Noise is what happens when we feel most fragile and unsettled within our own psyche. Would it not be better to calm our own agitation than to fight a losing battle against a world that will not go away?

happens when we cannot

welcome what we listen to.

Alienated from inner stillness,

we experience much of

the sound in our world as

an assault.

A distressed man went to his guru bemoaning the chaos of his life. "Babaji!" he cried, "my life is unbearable and getting worse all the time. We are so poor that my wife, my eight children, my in-laws and I have to live in a single room. We quarrel and get in each other's way. None of us can go on." The guru pondered and then made the villager promise to carry out his instructions. Desperate for salvation, the villager swore to do so. The guru asked the man what animals he owned and was told three cows, a goat, and a few hens that lived in the garden outside his hut. "Good," the guru said, "go home and bring them all into your hut." Inwardly aghast at the thought, the man promised. At sunrise he waited outside his guru's hut to wail more loudly about how much worse things were. With his house turned into a barn, his life was a living hell. "Son," said the guru, "go home and take the hens out of the house, life will improve." Again the next day he returned crying, "It's no good, the goat has eaten our food and our bedding. Please help me." "Go home," said the guru, "and put the goat in the garden. Life will get better." It wasn't long before the man again returned, complaining that the cows had kept him up at night. "You're absolutely right," said the guru. "Go home and put the cows in the field." The next day the villager returned, this time with his face beaming. "Guru, a thousand thanks. My house is peaceful again. What a **joy**."

When our own minds are so filled with thoughts, the sounds of the world compete with them for attention and for room. We go through our day distracted and torn between opposing forces, both our inner and outer worlds shouting for our attention. The solution, we think, is to do more, go faster, and speak more.

040 Thought in itself is no obstacle to silence.

When our own minds are so filled with thoughts, the sounds of the world compete with them for attention and for room. We go through our day distracted and torn between opposing forces, both our inner and outer worlds shouting for our attention. The solution, we think, is to do more, go faster, and **speak** more. The exhaustion we carry with us is the residue of the overactive mind.

Thought in itself is no obstacle to silence. Being lost in thought and confusion, inattentive, addicted to fantasy and daydreams and the endless speculation, conjecture, and evaluation that fill our minds—these are the obstacles to silence. We may be tempted to blame our mind for the noise we endure inwardly and attempt to subdue our thinking. We might believe that thought itself is our enemy. In fact, our thoughts **articulate** understanding and are vehicles of communication and creativity that are necessary to our lives. Our minds have within them the power to be the home of a profound

silence that does not depend upon the subduing or erasure of thought. The mind that is freed from agitation is a mind of both stillness and creativity.

The speed and the incessant nature of our thinking is at times just the visible face of deeper feelings of agitation and anxiety. Trying to subjugate, subdue, or control our minds does not heal those underlying wounds. It only makes an **opponent** of our minds, unjustly blamed for the chaos that overwhelms us. Learning to befriend our minds is born of learning to listen to our minds. Probing beneath the stories, concepts, judgments, and plans, we attend to the deeper rhythms of our hearts. We will not find a solution to noise through thinking about it or inventing more and more strategies to control it. Our experience of being **bombarded** by noise will not be healed by simply avoiding it. It is by learning to bring a gentle and loving attention to the voices clamoring in our minds that we will learn to heal and restore the fragmentation that lies beneath them.

Noise is sound that we do not feel in harmony with and so reject, struggle with, or deny. We will gladly attend to the sound of the owl outside our windows, yet find ourselves recoiling at the sound of the garbage truck coming down the street. We listen wholeheartedly to the voice of a friend we care for, yet find ourselves cringing at the sound of the colleague we dislike. If we are about to set out on a long-awaited journey, we listen with eager anticipation for the sound of the train's arrival. When saying farewell to someone we love, we hear the same sound with dread. If our heart is filled with serenity, there is little that can disturb us. Discovering genuine silence in our hearts, we discover there is little in the world that can be described as noise.

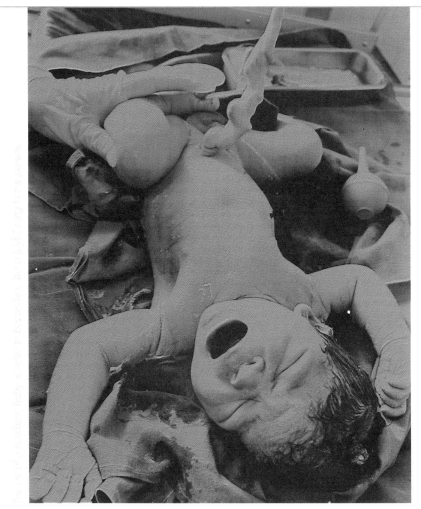

It is sound that teaches us the nature of silence.

There is no such thing as silence without sound.

The most direct path to silence is found when we turn our attention to everything we describe as noise. Listen wholeheartedly to the sounds that come to you through your day—the sounds of the traffic, the ringing of the telephones, the background conversations, the hum of your refrigerator. Listen to the sound of the rain against your windows, the song of the bird, the laugh of a child, your own heartbeat. Listen to each unique voice—judging nothing, rejecting nothing. Listen to each thought as if it were an honored guest.

As we listen carefully and without prejudice, we learn that the cry of a child is as necessary as the sound of our pulse. As we let our resistance fall away, we hear the songs of all sounds and the sound of silence. All that we are letting go of are the things that bring unnecessary clutter to our mind. There is no such thing as silence without sound. It is sound that teaches us the nature of silence. Wholeheartedly present within the world of sound, we learn to listen to the silence between the sounds. As we listen more deeply we hear the silence within the sounds. We discover within sound and silence a heart at peace with all things. We are taught and enriched by the sounds that come. Resting within the silence of our own hearts, we discover that silence is never far away but is perhaps the most essential dimension of consciousness. Within it speaks the gentle, clear wisdom of our heart.

it takes immense **courage**
to be willing to meet ourself in **silence** 044

Silence, we understand, is a definition of intimacy and

trust. The silent moments we share with people we love

and are deeply connected with are an expression of a

mutual acceptance, confidence, and understanding.

Silence is what frees us to listen well, to live with authenticity, and to discover wholeness within ourselves.

POSITIVE AND NEGATIVE

in silence we are visible to ourselves

Our personal relationship to

silence is best experienced through the simple experiment of sitting alone in a room, without any purpose or agenda, for half

an hour. Sit still, be quiet, and do nothing. Let yourself be bathed in silence, and in that still space just listen to what your

mind and heart do. You may experience a feeling of relief; nothing to accomplish, no one to look after, nothing that needs

attending to. How rare are those moments in our lives that are not filled with projects, lists, and tasks to be finished. You might find, in that silent space, that your body begins to soften and there is an enhanced **awareness** in how you see, hear, and feel. In just a short period of silent listening you may experience deeper levels of feeling and thought beginning to emerge. You may find yourself attuned to the places in your body, heart, or mind that feel burdened, wounded, or contracted. You may discover a greater sense of ease, born of the simple willingness to be still and attend to just the moment you are in.

After ten or twenty minutes you may also discover that the ease and relief you first welcomed so gratefully begin to change into something else. Feelings of edginess or

even anxiety may begin to creep in. You may decide that this is just boring, doing nothing, and find yourself reaching out to pick up a newspaper or hoping the telephone will ring. The habit of busyness begins to reassert itself. You begin to speculate on what a waste of time stillness is and that there is something much more productive you could be doing. You might even feel that you prefer distance and activity over sensing some of the wounded, tender places in your heart that begin to reveal themselves in silence.

Silence can be both **heaven** and hell; its depths and possibilities can be understood only through direct, personal experience. The 17th-century French philosopher and scientist Blaise Pascal wrote, "I have discovered that all of our unhappiness derives from one single source—not being able to sit quietly in a room."

We tend to have an ambivalent relationship with silence. Part of us, eager for self-discovery, insight, and possibility, hungers for the moments when we can listen more deeply. Part of us prefers the more familiar territory of our images, conclusions, and assumptions. We long for the serenity, peace, and balance silence seems to offer; we are equally infatuated with excitement, drama, and intensity. In silence we are visible to ourselves, no corner of our heart or mind is hidden or concealed. Silence is a way of being deeply honest with ourselves.

Silence can be both heaven and hell; its depths and possibilities can be understood only through direct, personal experience.

Can we find the inner silence that enables us to speak the words that truly connect us with another in a meaningful way? Can we find the inner silence that empowers us to speak the truths that need to be spoken? Can we find the silence that is vast enough to welcome the unknown and learn from it? Silence teaches us how to listen, to receive, and is the home of the most profound fearlessness.

Silence emerges when tension, struggle, and conflict fall away.

We long for this inner wholeness and self-understanding, yet fear being overwhelmed by the fears and uncertainties that may be revealed within us. We fear that silence may open the door to insecurities that we have locked away throughout our lives. In silence we are present with just what this **moment** offers and are invited to explore the richness of that invitation. We also come to realize how, much of our time, we have grown accustomed to living in the past or the future, seeking for something we have so far been unable to find in the present.

Silence, we understand, is a definition of intimacy and trust. The silent moments we share with people we love and are deeply connected with are an expression of a mutual **acceptance**, confidence, and understanding. When there is no fear between two people, silence becomes one of the most powerful mediums of communication. Silence emerges when tension, struggle, and conflict fall away. It is an expression of peace; when we are at peace with the world, our arguments with it dissolve into silence. When we start to learn to be at peace with ourselves, the agitation of our judgments, fears, and "shoulds," falls away. Silence is the embodiment of a profound harmony, which dissolves discord and division. Silence is joy, a **celebration** of life, and the home of revelation—the deeper understandings that restore us to wholeness and freedom.

Silence is also the birthplace of empathy and compassion. Learning to listen more deeply to ourself and the world, we emerge from times of silence with a deeper kindness, sensitivity, and openness to others. Listening deeply to the anguish of another person or the conflict of a community, we attune ourselves to the emotions and pain that lie beneath the words and actions of discord. In silence we learn to receive and welcome sorrow without fear or judgment. We come to understand through silence that in the moments of deep sorrow the greatest gift we can offer is that of heartfelt compassion.

Childhood memories of being

"hushed" are carried with us,

bringing with them the emotional

imprints of being punished,

devalued, and ignored.

Times of silence reveal to us the
equation that is made in our minds
between worth and activity.

It takes considerable courage to be silent. We may fear that silence will sentence us to a life in which we are invisible, unheard, unnoticed, and deemed to be unworthy. Childhood memories of being "hushed" are carried with us, bringing with them the emotional imprints of being punished, devalued, and ignored.

The power of those memories makes silence appear as dangerous, unpredictable, and threatening territory. Words become a way of reassuring ourselves that we are loved, wanted, and necessary. We come to believe that "I speak, therefore I am." At times we may even believe that shouting is the only way to attract the attention and love we need to bolster our self-confidence. We go to a party filled with unfamiliar faces, and find ourselves singing all our old songs, presenting our credentials and sharing our portfolios of life achievements. The old childhood mantra "Look at me" reasserts itself, seeking approval and affirmation. In the midst of anxiety it

is not always easy to give silence a chance. What does it feel like to enter into unfamiliar territory, the gatherings of unfamiliar faces and the new ventures with silence as a companion and an ally? Can we find the inner silence that enables us to speak the words that truly connect us with another in a meaningful way? Can we find the inner silence that empowers us to speak the truths that need to be spoken? Can we find the silence that is vast enough to welcome the unknown and learn from it?

Silence teaches us how to listen and to receive. It is the home of the most profound fearlessness. The history of all radical social and spiritual change teaches us that the most extraordinary and effective people in our world, those who have been pivotal to moments of profound social and political transformation, are those who are at ease in silence.

Times of silence reveal to us the equation that is made in our mind between worth and activity. When we are not producing, doing, and acting, we feel deprived of any evidence that we are a worthwhile human being.

Our way of introducing ourselves to another person frequently begins with the question, "What do you do?" How rarely do we ask, "Who are you?"

We can learn to nurture in our lives a sacred stillness.

Productivity, activity, and busyness become the central vocation in our life, consuming our time and attention to the extent that we forget how to listen to the quieter voices of our spirit—the voices that tell us that there is more to us than what we produce. Culturally, we have come to measure value and worth by the evidence of what we do and accomplish. Young children are torn from the innocence of their childhoods with the repeated interrogation, "What are you going to be when you grow up?"

Our way of introducing ourselves to another person frequently begins with the question, "What do you do?" How rarely do we ask, "Who are you?" If we cannot define ourselves apart from our credentials, it is difficult to understand another person in a deeper way. Accomplishment is equated with approval, respect, and belonging, so we drive ourselves more and more relentlessly in search of acceptability, often destroying our capacity for serenity and stillness in the process.

We can learn to nurture in our lives a sacred stillness that increasingly reveals vitality, creativity, and depth of spirit. The busiest among us benefit from moments of "divine inaction." Deep down we acknowledge that at the moment of our death it is not all of our accomplishments and credentials that will sustain and nourish us. Everything we have created and produced in this life will fade away. Do we truly wish the words "Here lies a person who produced a lot" to be etched upon our gravestone? Would we not wish to be remembered as a person of kindness, to leave behind us in our lives a legacy of peace, generosity, and wisdom? We can learn to use the lessons that death teaches us in our lives about how to live, remembering what is truly important and what genuinely makes a difference in our world.

Greatness of spirit grows in the silence and depths of our being. It asks us to find a home in silence. We find the path to peace in our life, relationships, and world when we learn how to be at peace with ourselves.

The gifts of great compassion, generosity, and stillness are born in our own hearts. The depth of who we are can never be measured by the accolades and achievements we gather, but through the vastness, **freedom**, and integrity we discover inwardly. In moments of silence our attention is naturally turned inward. Initially we may feel disoriented and lost. Our patterns of busyness reinstate themselves, and we think that there is something we should "do" with silence. We come to understand that silence is not something we create, not a project or a mission to be developed, and not a strategy applied to a "problem." As we learn to befriend silence, increasingly we understand that it has always awaited us. It is benevolent, a place of ease, free from judgment, demand, and expectation. We learn to sink into silence, to be bathed by it and understand its immense power to heal, restore, renew, and empower us. Silence invites us to surrender our illusion of being in **control**—of our mind, our emotions, our world. This can be truly frightening. We associate not being in control with being out of control, with anarchy and disorder. As we listen to our mind, we discover we cannot decide to have only pleasant, exciting thoughts, images, and memories. As we listen to our bodies, we discover that we cannot **command** them to have only the sensations we desire. As we listen to our hearts, we hear the whole spectrum of our emotional life arising and passing according to its own rhythms.

We are not "making" things happen. Neither are things happening "to us." It is just life that is happening, the countless births and deaths within every moment. This can be a truly shocking revelation to us. We are tempted to flee from this understanding and reassert our sense of control by "doing" something. Silence reveals a great vulnerability as we understand that we do not have the power to govern even our own mind, let alone the

Silence asks for a quality of surrender that is the antithesis of the philosophy, often central in our thinking that tells us that control is equivalent to safety. It is vulnerability that allows us to open our hearts and receive with tenderness and compassion all of the inner and outer activities of our life.

the great

It is vulnerability that allows us to be touched and moved by the sorrow and pain in our world. It is inner balance and strength that enable us to respond to those near us and those far from us with a genuine, heartfelt sensitivity and love.

world. Silence also reveals an innate strength and balance within us. We learn to be still amid all the changes, to receive them and to be taught by them. Silence asks for a quality of surrender that is the antithesis of the philosophy, often central in our thinking, that tells us that control is equivalent to safety. It is actually vulnerability that allows us to open our hearts and **receive**, with tenderness and compassion, all of the inner and outer activities of our life. It is vulnerability that allows us to be touched and moved by the sorrow and pain in our world. It is inner balance and strength that enable us to respond to those near us and those far from us with a genuine, heartfelt sensitivity and love.

Surrendering our notions of control reveals the peace born of living in harmony with the way life actually is. Despite our most strenuous efforts, we cannot make anything in this world conform to our wishes, fantasies, or desires. Even the most **heroic** exertions fail to make one single thing last or endure, or succeed in banishing the unpleasant and challenging from our life. The very nature of life means that we will continue to be exposed to the whole spectrum of delightful and sorrowful, **affirming** and shattering, painful and pleasant experiences that life holds. With control, all that we do is futilely endeavor to separate ourselves from the very nature and heart of life. In silence we learn to connect more profoundly with life's rhythms. We discover within ourselves the serenity, and strength to experience our life fully and directly.

In silence we make an appointment with aloneness. The mystics and the sages

Taking our tentative steps into silence, we learn to befriend it and to befriend ourselves. It teaches us to listen, to see ourselves with new eyes, and to enter our life with a profound receptivity. As we learn to embrace silence we come to understand that, in truth, we have always been embraced by silence. It is the gateway we enter to find true depth, intimacy, and wisdom.

To be intimate with another person, to live together in a peaceful and compassionate way, we first need to understand how to heal and care for ourself. It is our relationship with ourself that is the foundation of every other relationship in our life.

of the past and present never took with them on their pilgrimage a crowd of companions, projects to engage in if they became bored, or a cellphone in case they became lonely. Silence is a **journey** we make in solitude, and it is not always an easy one. Sitting in a silent room for just half an hour, we are at times horrified by our craving for distraction and fear of facing ourselves. The multitude of often diversionary activities with which we fill our day serves to camouflage our fear of aloneness.

Solitude is often equated with loneliness, deprivation, unworthiness, or being unlovable. At times solitude reveals painful **inner** feelings of being incomplete and our need to be with people to feel at ease. Our minds rush in a desperate search to find reassurance and consolation. Silence is an initiation into a solitude of peace and wholeness. It is never a rejection of our essential relatedness and connection with people and with life. It is instead the training ground of true relationship.

The most profound lessons of our lives we learn alone, and no one can substitute for us in this learning. Alone we learn how to let go, to embrace sorrow, to listen to ourselves, and to make **peace** with the whole range of anxieties, needs, and feelings that we carry. Alone we learn the lessons of compassion, generosity, and forgiveness. No one outside of ourselves can teach us how to make peace with ourselves, to find meaning in our life, or to shed the burdens of regret or sorrow that live within us. We can never truly understand ourselves through the eyes of another. It takes immense courage to be willing to meet ourself in silence. The journey into silence is a commitment we make to ourselves. It may be the deepest gift of compassion and love we could ever offer ourselves. Alone we learn how to tend to ourselves, to understand what it is we may need to let go of to live in a freer and fuller way. Alone we come to understand what qualities of heart we may need to nurture to heal and restore ourselves to wholeness.

As human beings we need, perhaps more than anything else, to know how to touch one another. We are undeniably related and interconnected; we depend upon each other in countless ways we do not always even see. To be intimate with another person, to live together in a peaceful and compassionate way, we first need to understand how to heal and care for ourself. It is our relationship with ourself that is the **foundation** of every other relationship in our life. Here we learn the lessons of kindness rather than harshness. Within our relationship with ourself we learn how to be a cause of healing and not a cause of harm. Within the world of our own heart, body, and mind we learn a generosity of spirit, trust, and sensitivity that we can bring to every relationship in our life. Alienated from ourselves we will always be prone to loneliness in our lives. Learning the richness and ease of aloneness we discover what it means to be whole: "all one." Genuine connectedness is not born of the glancing encounters with the multitude of people in our world, but through our capacity to enter into each moment and each relationship with trust, **openness**, and generosity.

Silence appears as dangerous territory only so long as it remains a stranger to us. It appears threatening only from a distance; we fear it only as long as we fear knowing ourselves. Taking our tentative steps into silence, we learn that we can befriend it and so befriend ourselves. It teaches us to listen to our inner intuition, to see ourselves with new eyes and to enter our life with a profound receptivity. As we **learn** to embrace silence, we come to understand that, in truth, we have always been embraced by silence. It is the gateway we enter to find true depth, intimacy, and wisdom.

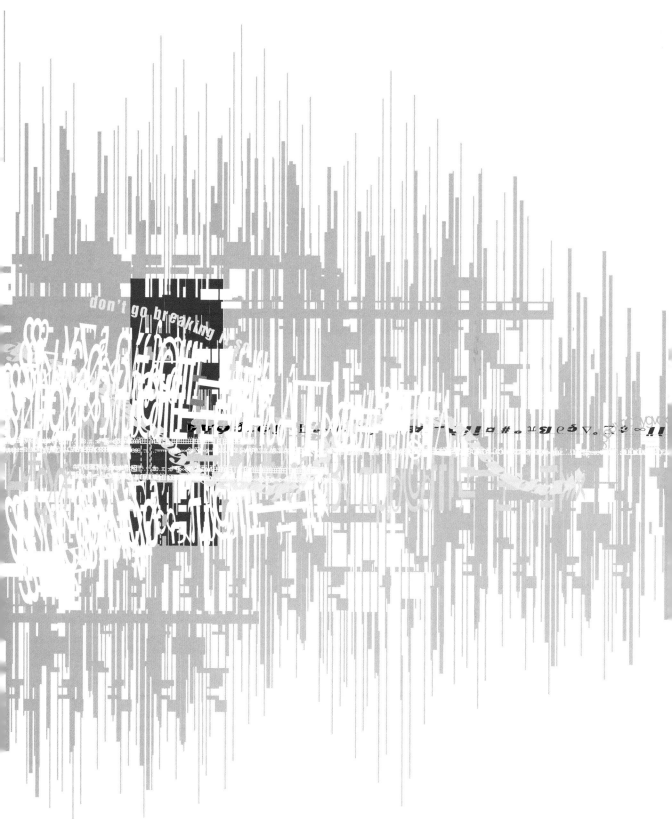

don't go breaking

2

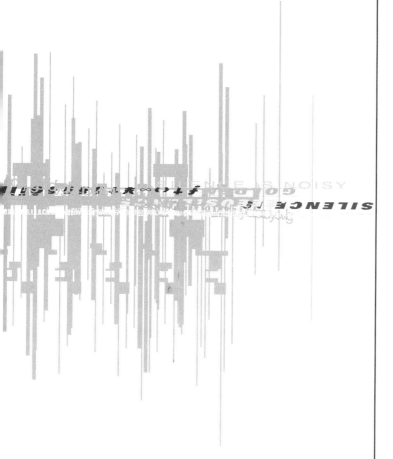

SILENCE IS NOISY

GOLD で買う
SILENCE IS

calming our **minds**

we begin to calm our **world**

Words pour from our mouths, sometimes saying little but serving only to cover up uncomfortable silences. Words of harshness, judgment, or blame spill forth and can never be recovered.

The discovery and reclaiming of silence is a path and an art. We are learning to still the turbulence of our hearts. We are discovering what it means to be at peace with ourselves.

FIRST STEPS ON THE WAY

> time is both a tyrant and an idol

Ancient mystics and sages retreated from the world, renounced familial responsibilities, and embraced solitude as the path to the discovery of inner richness and solitude. We may not be drawn to the austerity of this withdrawal, yet may feel in our own heart an urgent need for greater stillness, peace, and depth. We do not need to abandon the world, our families, or responsibilities to begin to taste the sweetness of silence. We may need to learn the art of creating an oasis of stillness and calm within the clamor and haste of our own lives. This is a very personal journey. Only we, ourselves, can know the places and moments when we become lost in agitation, anxiety, turmoil, and disconnection. These are the very places that cry out for our attention, that call for transformation, and offer the greatest possibilities of new ways of being. In the midst of agitation we can learn to bring calmness; in the midst of alienation we can begin to foster intimacy; in the places of greatest struggle we can explore the possibility of serenity; and in turmoil we can find tranquillity. We cannot always control the speed of our world and the people in it—we can choose how we engage with it and respond to it.

We can all create sanctuaries of stillness in our days.

To transform our entire lives is too immense a task; to expect ourselves to change the habits of a lifetime in a day is too daunting; to demand of ourselves that the clamor of our minds should abruptly end is unrealistic and unhelpful. We need to think of the discovery of silence as a path that asks of us consistent, kind attention and care. It is a path that we can learn to travel in the midst of our daily lives and activities, step by step.

tune in to the · emotional tones of · the inner voices that · clamor for attention · simply noticing · where there is · anxiety, agitation · anticipation · resistance or need · Explore what it · means to listen · without being lost · not chasing after · any of the thoughts · not trying to banish · them, subdue them, · or modify them

What difference would it make in our lives if we were to give as much time and attention to the cultivation of calmness and stillness as we give to producing and doing?

Each moment of our lives is worthy of our wholehearted attention, each moment holds the possibility of new ways of seeing and being. Each time we turn toward the busiest and most agitated moments and places in our lives with the willingness to find calmness, sensitivity, and stillness within them, we are taking a significant step on the path to silence. As we travel this path there will be countless moments when we find ourselves reverting to habitual modes of agitation and haste or becoming lost in the busyness of our life and mind.

These countless moments are equally the countless invitations we have to begin again, to feel our feet on the ground, to listen to the sounds of the world. What difference would it make in our lives if we were to give as much time and attention to the cultivation of calmness and stillness as we give to producing and doing? It is a common mistake to assume that activity is more important and valuable than stillness.

We can all create sanctuaries of stillness in our days. These are precious moments of "sacred idleness" in which we reconnect with ourselves, our deepest values, and the landscape of our heart and mind. Born of these sanctuaries of stillness is the clear awareness that it is possible for us to make wise choices about how we live, what we dedicate ourselves to, and the quality of our lives.

We can learn what it means to live an intentional life, rather than an "accidental" life governed by circumstance, demand, expectation, and anxiety. An intentional life is one in which the activities we engage in are an embodiment of the sensitivity, compassion, and intimacy that we have learned to treasure in our hearts.

Creating sanctuaries of silence does not require immense amounts of time and effort. It would be unhelpful to approach stillness as yet another task. The fostering of stillness is a gift we offer to ourselves, a time of healing and renewal and of nurturing spiritual depth. We are

We can all learn to calm down, slow down, listen more
deeply, and attend to the well-being of our heart and mind.

engaged in the awakening of our heart, our capacity
to love deeply and live fully. There is probably no more
precious gift that we could ever be offered.
We can all learn to calm down, slow down, listen
more deeply, and attend to the well-being of our heart and
mind. The Chilean poet Pablo Neruda wrote in his poem
"Keeping Quiet:"

> "If we were not so single-minded
>
> about keeping our lives moving,
>
> and for once could do nothing,
>
> perhaps a huge silence
>
> might interrupt this sadness
>
> of never understanding ourselves."

Silence is never far away

Explore what it means to listen without being lost.

What difference would it make in the quality of our life if we were to take a time in the beginning and ending of our day that was simply dedicated to stillness? In those moments experiment with intentionally creating a sanctuary of silence. In the morning, before you begin the activities of your day, take a few moments when you leave the television turned off, the phone unplugged, the dishes unwashed, and the radio silent.

Explore purposefully what it means to be still, while having no particular purpose at all. Let your body and mind relax, and dedicate the time to simply **listening** with as much sensitivity and wholeheartedness as you can muster. Experiment with bringing a gentle and curious awareness to everything that is happening in your body. Explore what it means simply to be awake to the life of your body with all its sensations, its places of tightness and places of **ease**, and feeling the contact of your feet with the floor or your back on the chair.

Bring the same sensitivity to listen to the landscape of your mind and heart. Tune in to the emotional tones of the inner voices that clamor for your attention, simply noticing where there is anxiety, agitation, anticipation, **resistance**, or need. Explore what it means to listen without being lost— not chasing after any of the thoughts, not trying to control them, subdue them, or modify them. Exploring silence, we discover a refuge that is always available to us.

At the end of your day, experiment once more with a few moments of dedicated stillness. Instead of trying to **camouflage** the tensions and residues accumulated in the day with distraction, input, entertainment, or yet more busyness, once more dedicate some time to listening to yourself. As you turn your attention to your body, soften the places that have accumulated tension through the day. Taking these moments to attend to the life of your **mind** and heart, you may be stunned to discover the number and intensity of thoughts that swirl through your consciousness.

Attend to the life of your mind and heart.

In the marketplace of our lives we learn to return to silence, and appreciate that our capacity to live at ease in silence is the ultimate birthplace of our creativity and effectiveness.

In our busy minds, conversations and encounters replay themselves in a perpetual loop; disappointments or frustrations appear, demanding attention. We are experiencing the extraordinary pressure of a mind bowed beneath the weight of its accumulated impressions. It is an uncomfortable experience; we are tempted to flee from ourselves or to submerge the discomfort in distraction. We also become acutely aware that the two things we cannot divorce ourselves from in this life are our own minds and hearts. Embracing this understanding deeply, we know the urgency of caring for the quality of our mind and heart.

Instead of fleeing from or avoiding the chaos of our psychological, emotional landscape, we learn to bring a gentle, clear attentiveness to it. The most direct way to transformation of the heart is to turn directly toward those inner places that are the most wounded and chaotic. We cannot always blame the world, our responsibilities, or ourselves for the inner chaos and noise that feel so unendurable. We begin to understand that the inner turmoil is a result of the many moments of incomplete attention we've brought to the encounters of our day, the inner agitation that has compelled us to haste, and the times we have become simply lost in our expectations, wants, plans, and thoughts. All of this can be transformed as we deeply understand that a life of engagement, activity, and creativity does not preordain a sentence of agitation and anxiety.

Mindfulness asks us not to rush through the day, but to relish each moment.

The moments of **stillness** we gift to ourselves are powerful symbols that remind us of the power of silence and communion. We listen to our cascading thoughts without judging, rejecting, or blaming, and our minds respond to the kindness of this attention. The clamor of the thoughts begins to slow, the grip of the agitation begins to be released, and we again glimpse inner calm and silence, which are truly **healing** and creative. We all need these moments of remembering what our work and our life are truly about, what we value most deeply, and

We listen to our cascading thought without judging, rejecting or blaming and our minds respond to the kindness of this attention.

The world shows us as much beauty as we are able to see.

who we are, apart from our roles and activities. We are all restored and renewed through these moments dedicated to "doing nothing" and remembering what it means to "be."

We live in a world of **symbols** that endeavor primarily to convince us of the virtue of having more, becoming more, and producing more. Absorbing these messages as the guidelines we live by, we are compelled into more and more busyness and frequently into being increasingly alienated from ourselves and the quiet wisdom of our hearts. Dedicated times of stillness in our days are powerful reminders for us to return to ourselves, to treasure silence, and to understand that we cannot truly measure ourselves by what we have gained in this life. The depth of our being may be more truly measured by what we have been able to let go of.

Silence is not a geographical place, nor is it dependent upon removing ourselves from the world. Silence is never far away from us. Our **challenge** is to untangle the habits of haste and restlessness that can

_____ We are learning to be at peace with all things, to untangle the habits of haste and restlessness that can govern our lives.

We live in a world of symbols that endeavour primarily to convince us of the virtue of having more becoming more and producing more. Absorbing these messages as the guidelines we live by, we are compelled into more and more busyness and frequently into being increasingly alienated from ourselves and the quiet wisdom of our hearts.

Awareness helps us see the beauty of our world.

govern our lives. As we begin to appreciate the richness of silence, we may also become increasingly aware of the many moments we habitually fill with distraction or activity. These are the very moments that invite us to pause, to rest in "not doing" and discover the inner ease available to us. We learn to pay attention to those in-between moments when we wait for a bus, stand in line, sit in a traffic jam, or unexpectedly discover an empty space in our appointment calendar.

These moments offer the option of exploring the different pathways available to us. We can reach out for a magazine, fume and complain, shout at the world, or squeeze in one more telephone conversation. We can regard these moments as wasted time or appreciate them as moments when nothing specific is asked of us and savor the stillness and ease. Instead of floundering in frustration, impatience, or agitation, we can allow ourselves to be silent, to listen with clear attention to our inner and outer worlds. We may close our eyes or simply look with appreciation at the sights around us. We may bring our attention to all the sensations in our bodies, to the touch of our feet on the ground and the wind on our cheek, and simply be present in the life of our body.

In all of the events and activities of our lives we can explore what it means to create a "sacred space." There are those who complain that they have no time to be still, no time to nurture silence, no time to "be." Time has become a tyrant and an idol in our lives. With so much to do, and become, we regard time as a commodity to be revered and filled. Do we have time to breathe, to walk, to feel, to think, and to see? We all have this— and so we have time to be silent. In the marketplace of our lives we learn to return to silence, treasure silence, and appreciate that our capacity to be at ease in silence is the ultimate birthplace of true creativity and effectiveness.

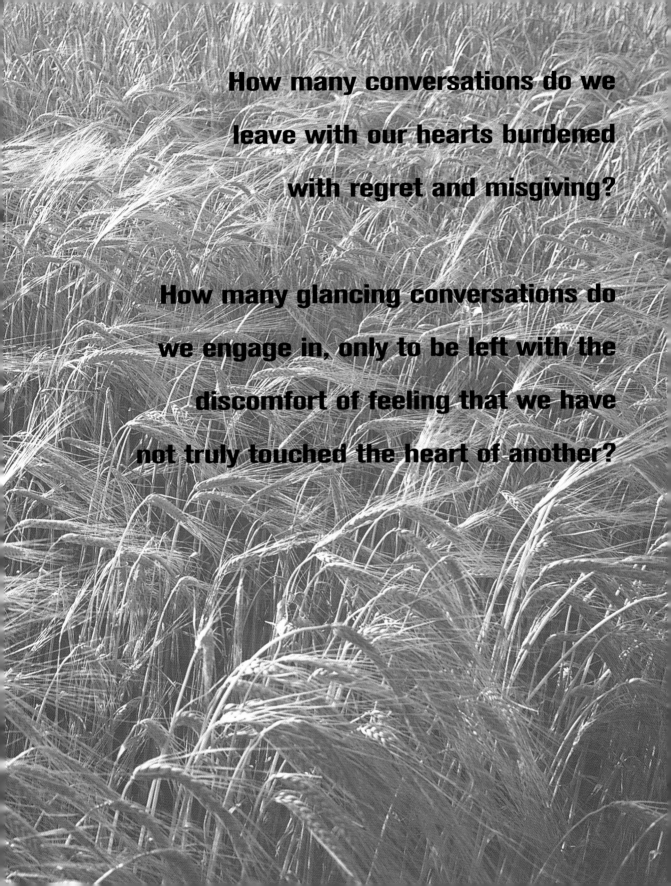

How many conversations do we leave with our hearts burdened with regret and misgiving?

How many glancing conversations do we engage in, only to be left with the discomfort of feeling that we have not truly touched the heart of another?

Endless chatter fills our days, often just to console us that we are not alone in this world.

The discovery of silence is an experiment undertaken in the classroom of our life.

nificant areas of living that is truly enhanced by silence is within the countless conversations that fill our d

What difference would it make to eat one meal a day in silence, truly savoring and appreciating the food that we eat? When we sit in the busyness of a restaurant, instead of reaching out for a book or starting a conversation, can we approach that moment as a time of wholehearted listening? What difference would it make in our life for one week or even for one day to renounce hurrying? Instead of rushing from our home in the morning and then perpetuating the agitation of hurrying from one event to another through our day, we can begin our day with the intention of moving with more calmness and sensitivity.

The discovery of silence is an experiment undertaken in the classroom of our life. Agitation and restlessness, born of underlying anxiety and alienation, are the opponents of silence. Activity and engagement in all the events of our lives do not separate us from silence. As we begin to discover silence within ourselves, we begin to discover it in all the events of our lives. In a busy law office in New York new employees are often startled to discover that part of their contract includes a commitment to begin each day with ten minutes of silence. The team meets, hierarchies and briefcases momentarily set aside. The director of the office asserts that employees who value inner peace, calmness, and stillness are employees who not only value themselves but manifest the capacity to approach their clients with greater compassion and effectiveness.

One highly significant area of living that is truly enhanced by silence is the countless conversations that fill our days. Meaningful, clear, and effective speech is born of our capacity to be at ease in silence. Compassionate, wise, and kind speech grows from our ability to listen silently to another. Busyness and agitation are manifest not only in our actions but also in our speech. Words pour from our mouths, sometimes saying little and serving only to cover up uncomfortable silences. Words of harshness,

Compassionate, wise, and kind speech grows from our ability to listen silently to another.

The most intimate, meaningful connections and relationships we form in our life are those that flourish as well in silence as in words.

...eaningful, clear, and effective speech is born of our capacity to be at ease in silence. Compassionate, w...

judgment, or blame spill forth and can never be recovered. Endless chatter fills our days, often just to console us that we are not alone in this world. How many conversations do we leave with our hearts burdened with regret and misgiving? How many glancing conversations do we engage in, only to be left with the discomfort of feeling that we have not truly touched the heart of another?

The degree of ease with silence

that we begin to discover inwardly is the measure of ease that we start to find in our connections with other people. Our chatter tends to be an ongoing replay of the conclusions, assumptions, and opinions we have already formed. As we learn to be more silent, we also learn to listen more deeply and understand both ourselves and others in new ways. Silence is not the absence of speech but the growing capacity to be mindful within speech. We learn to listen to what lies beneath the words, the feelings and moods swirling within us. We begin to find

the wisdom in speaking what is true, meaningful, and needed. A wise person in this world is one who knows not only when to speak but also how to listen. The most meaningful connections and relationships we form in our life are those that flourish equallly as well in silence as in words.

The discovery and reclaiming of silence

is a path and an art. We are learning to still the turbulence of our hearts. We are discovering what it means to be at peace with ourselves. Calming our minds, we begin to calm our world. Silence is an art that asks for attention and dedication. The commuter on the train and the hermit on the mountaintop face the same challenge—to calm the waves of agitation and anxiety that lead them to flee from themselves and the present moment. To discover the peace of silence, the path also needs to be one of peace and calmness. We are not seeking, in our quest for silence, to vanquish, overcome, or abandon ourselves. We are learning to be at peace with all things.

listen to the moments of **silence**

fear of change, fear of **silence**

Mindful attention is a force that brings into consciousness

everything that has previously been unconscious, illuminates what

has been hidden, and directly connects us with the vitality of our

body, mind, heart, and the changing textures of each moment.

The lure of the past and the future is powerful, and the habit of busyness is enticing.

THE NEW ROOM

befriending silence

When we move into a new home our first hours are often dedicated to hanging the familiar pictures, arranging the furniture in recognizable patterns and making sure that the telephone is connected. We do all that we can to transform a house into a home that we feel at ease in and can call our own. As we begin to explore the nature of silence we are invited to question what it is that we need to leave behind so that we can feel at home within it. We may be tempted to move the **familiar** furniture of our **mind** into the times in our day that we dedicate to silence. Sitting quietly, alone with ourselves for even brief periods, we see our inclination to fill that time with fantasy, rehearsals, daydreams, and the endless loops of oft-repeated conversations. The lure of the past and the future is powerful, and the habit of busyness is enticing.

The task of learning to be intimate with silence asks us to learn new lessons of patience, dedication, sensitivity, and simplicity. Initially, silence looks like a vast, empty space, which unsettles us and leads us to want to flee into

The deeper, pivotal questions we have carried with us through our life about the nature of freedom, the sacred, love, and peace will not be answered by more knowledge and thought, but through our willingness to descend into silence.

For the richness and depth of silence to unfold, each one of us needs to learn how to let go of the familiar strategies and formulas that have guided us in our life. In learning how to let go of the layers of busyness and preoccupation that absorb our attention, we learn to listen to the moments of silence and all that they can teach us.

journey of spiritual
depth and richness

more familiar territory. We become acutely aware of what is **missing** in silence—the roles and identities that reassure us of our worth, the consolation and affirmation that are sought through our relationships and all the activity we rely upon to provide meaning in our life.

Silence invites us to understand who we are apart from all that we have accumulated and achieved in our lives. In allowing ourselves to be still, we are learning to nurture a more intuitive, direct, truthful way of seeing ourselves and the world. The deeper, pivotal questions we have carried with us through our life about the nature of freedom, the **sacred**, love, and peace will not be answered by more knowledge and thought, but through our willingness to descend into silence.

Silence is unfamiliar territory, a new room we are learning to be intimate with. Each time we enter into periods of silence we are following in the footsteps of the ancient masters and mystics. We are taking a step into an uncharted dimension, the unknown, and undertaking a path with no obvious guarantees. What guides us is a quiet, recurrent inner longing for wholeness and peace that cannot be ignored. Embracing silence, we learn the same lesson that every pilgrim of the past has been asked to learn. For the **richness** and depth of silence to unfold, each one of us needs to learn how to let go of the familiar strategies and formulas that have guided us in our life. In learning how to let go of the layers of busyness that absorb our attention, we learn to listen to the moments of silence and all that they can teach us.

Nurturing an inner environment of silence is supported by finding both a place and time in which we can consciously disconnect from busyness. It is enough simply to dedicate a corner of a room to being a space of simplicity and stillness. Creating a **temple** in your home is not complex. Remove the clutter, close the door, discard the distractions, and you have everything you need

The pose and alertness we cultivate in our posture encourage us to discover the same steadiness and alertness in our mind and heart.

Silence is an art, and like any other art it requires effort and engagement.

It is enough simply to dedicate a corner of a room to being a space of simplicity and stillness. Creating a temple in your home is not complex.

Silence enables a slow but powerful transformation

to be alone and still, and to begin to attend to the deeper rhythms of life. Introducing into our physical environment a space that is devoted to stillness is a powerful metaphor that reminds us to attend to the most important quest in our lives—the journey of spiritual depth and richness. What a great difference it would make in our lives to return home after a day of busyness and activity to be greeted by a reminder to come back to ourselves, to let go, and to find renewal. Visit the space you create many times in a day, for a few minutes or longer. Experiment with just being at ease and learning to rest in "non-doing," with no demands or tasks to answer. Use this uncluttered space as a reminder of the inner worth to be found in silence, and keep it free from mess and disorder. Through silence we learn to treat our own inner space in the same way.

The sacred space we create in our home is dedicated to being truly awake. Initially, if we approach it fatigued and exhausted by our day, we

may tend to find ourselves sinking into weariness or disconnection. Silence is an art, and like any other art it requires effort and engagement. As you take your seat in the temple you have created, pay attention to your posture. Find a position that is an expression of alertness and wakefulness without straining. Let your back and neck be upright, feel the touch of your feet on the floor and then consciously soften all the areas of tension or tightness in your face, hands, shoulders, and belly.

Waves of restlessness may appear in your body as you engage with silence. You may notice your eyes hungrily beginning to wander around the room searching for distraction; let your eyes gently close. Restlessness often first appears in our hands; they begin to flutter, scratch, and wander—let your hands be still and feel them resting on your body. The poise and alertness we cultivate in our posture encourage us to discover the same steadiness and alertness in our mind and heart.

this

moment,

this body,

and this

mind

our attention jumps from the past to the future, replays one event after another, speculates, worries, and judges

We are learning one of the most significant and transforming lessons of life: how to let go, to let things be and be wholeheartedly present.

Calming our own mind and heart, we are learning the ways to bring calmness into each moment of our life

The restlessness we encounter in our body has its origin in the restlessness of our mind. Stripping ourselves of distraction, even for brief periods, we begin to experience the remarkably unsettled and fretful nature of our minds. Our attention jumps from the past to the future, replays one event after another, speculates, worries, and judges. Peace and **stillness** seem far away as we find ourselves drowning in the torrent of thoughts and images that flood our minds. Being alone and still can initially be a deeply uncomfortable experience. Rocked by the inner waves of busyness, we are tempted to run from silence.

The journey into silence invites us to reverse the trend of disconnection and agitation that has the **power** to alienate us from life, other people, and ourselves. Instead of fleeing from ourself, we can learn simply to come back—to this moment, this body, and this mind. There is not a better or more perfect moment for us to discover silence than this moment we are in. We are learning to live a life of presence rather than a life of postponement, in which silence is projected into some future time when the demands and events of living have calmed. Each moment we become lost in the flood of thinking and restlessness, we can come back, we can begin again. Each time we do this, we are **learning** one of the most significant and transforming lessons of life: how to let go, to let things be and be wholeheartedly present. In the moments we are tempted to jump up from our seat and pursue the endless possibilities of activity and preoccupation, we need to remind ourselves that there is nothing more worthy of our attention than our own well-being and peace. When we are governed by **agitation**, it is agitation we bring to every encounter and event in our life. Calming our own mind and heart, we are learning the ways to bring calmness into each moment of our life. Learning to come back to the simplicity and stillness of this moment requires profound patience. We can begin anew in each moment.

In the moments when we step out of the activity of our life and into this new territory of stillness, we may discover cellular levels of fatigue we have previously been unaware of. Taking your seat in stillness, you may find yourself sinking into sleepiness or a kind of mental fog. The weariness you experience may be just the depths of tiredness that surface as you listen to the life of your body. Exhaustion and tiredness can also be a way of disconnection, retreating from unpleasant feelings and thoughts. In stillness we sometimes come across the deep reluctance we have to just be with ourselves. Silence and aloneness may carry for us shadows of deprivation and anxiety. The clouds of tiredness and fog we sometimes encounter serve to distance us from deeply experiencing those feelings we fear. If you sense that the sleepy, clouded mind is a familiar pathway of disconnection, experiment with taking a few deep breaths, or bring your attention to all the sensations flowing through your body. This is a way of sharpening your attention and probing beneath the surface of the numbing fog.

Silence is a mirror in which we can learn to see our life and self reflected clearly.

Silence is a mirror in which we and all of life are revealed. When we are silent, we hear and see more acutely and so approach the gateway of understanding. We are engaged in a gentle exploration of the lessons that silence offers and are learning to be at home and at ease in this unfamiliar territory. As we accustom ourselves to being more silent, we discover that with patience and gentle attention the whirlwind of our mind begins to slow and calm. We begin to see our thoughts and the images that fill our minds objectively, as if from a distance. We can listen to the story they tell us about the disappointments, dreams, fears, and hopes that live in our hearts. We learn to attend to the many inner voices, with all their different melodies of harshness, compassion, anxiety, trust, judgment, and forgiveness. Within all these different **voices** we begin to discern what nurtures us and what undermines us, what contributes to pain and alienation and what heals us. We learn about the qualities we need and what it would be helpful for us to let go of.

Befriending silence requires not just attention but compassionate attention. We encounter the powerful voices of frustration, "should," expectation, fear, and demand. It is tempting to judge, to berate ourselves and so further perpetuate the powerful cycles of agitation and discontent. We come to believe we should be different, want to be different, and fantasize about who we need to become. So accustomed are we to accepting that activity, will, and effort are the only means to effect change, we may find it difficult to comprehend that some of the deepest transformations of our hearts will occur in the alchemy of silence. As we listen to the many, often disappointing and discordant, voices of our heart, we can learn to **restrain** ourselves from the familiar and habitual pathways of strategies, judgment, and activity. We long for transformation, perhaps even becoming ambitious about transformation, sometimes forgetting that genuine, enduring transformation is born only of true acceptance and **compassion**. Silence is not a way of fixing the past or strategizing the future, it is a way of being simply present. We learn to greet and welcome the many voices of our heart not with resignation, despair, or rejection but with genuine openness and sensitivity.

Silence changes us, transforms us, and connects us with what we treasure most deeply. It teaches us to let go of all of our preconceived ideas, assumptions, conclusions, and images. In silence we become increasingly mindful of each thought, feeling, sensation and story that ripples through us, and we learn what it means to be awake to our life and ourself. This is magical in itself. All of the changes we long for in our life begin with a change of heart. Instead of meandering endlessly in clouds of habit, we learn to be awake and present. Instead of abandoning ourselves in distraction and busyness, we learn the wisdom of listening. Compassion begins in each moment we are willing to receive the world and ourself without blame or **prejudice**.

Patience, compassion, the commitment to stillness, and the willingness to begin anew in each moment are all ingredients in the awakening of our heart.

The habits of our mind and heart begin to soften and dissolve in the light of affectionate, mindful attention.

Befriending silence is, in fact, a process of learning to befriend ourselves. The habits of our mind and heart begin to soften and dissolve in the light of affectionate, mindful attention. The attention we cultivate in silence illuminates all the details of our moment-to-moment experience.

Through attention we establish ourselves in the simplicity of one moment at a time. Mindful attention is a force that brings into consciousness everything that has previously been UNCONSCIOUS, illuminates what has been hidden, and directly connects us with the vitality of our body, mind, heart, and the changing textures of each moment. Attention is simple, but it is not always easy. Each time we pause in our life, we are building a bridge to silence. Patience, compassion, the commitment to stillness, and the willingness to begin anew in each moment are all ingredients in the awakening of our heart. Through mindful attention, we are learning to care for ourselves and our world in the deepest way possible.

Genuine peace is discovered in the midst of agitation; true compassion is born in the turmoil of pain; fearlessness is found in our willingness to explore the fears and anxieties that shadow us.

What is it that makes our hearts sing? What do we truly long for and value? What does it mean to be free and live an authentic life? Initially, we may find ourselves desperately searching for a definitive answer to these questions to solve the anxiety they provoke.

AGONY AND ECSTASY

life changes—moment to moment

Silent retreats continue to occupy a central role in the great spiritual traditions of our world. Countless people take time out of the preoccupations of their lives to spend days or weeks on retreat. Retreats are **environments** dedicated to inner renewal, spiritual depth, and caring for the well-being of heart and mind. Many people discover that they need these times without **responsibilities** or demands, so that the chatter and fixations of their minds can exhaust themselves, allowing the reclamation of inner stillness and calm. Silent retreats offer the opportunity for us to take our place in the timeless traditions of enclosure, contemplation, and transformation.

Novices to retreats often find themselves anticipating these periods of seclusion as guarantors of bliss, elation, spiritual ecstasy, and profound revelation. We formulate romantic, exciting images of what will happen to us in the days or weeks of silence we undertake. Experiences of **profound** bliss, serenity, and joy are hoped for, even expected. It is not unusual, after a few days on retreat, for those same people to find themselves plotting routes of escape.

Whenever we undertake periods of silence and contemplation, we leave behind us the familiar territory of our routines, habits, and the various ways we order and control our world and enter unfamiliar territory. Taking that step into uncharted territory, we leave behind not only the familiar structures of our life but also the reassurance and consolation we draw from them. Newcomers on retreats find a certain relief in verbal silence.

nce is a place of mystery. We cannot predict what will emerge

fold. Moments of darkness and sweetness live in silence

The tradition of silence is in a very real way intended to disturb us—to stretch our psychological, emotional, and spiritual horizons

we may feel panic—almost as if starved of air

Within hours or days the same silence can reveal a deep sense of **deprivation**. We become acutely aware of the extent we use words to prevent us from feeling alone and isolated.

Silence, we soon discover, deprives us of the reassurance and security we derive from verbal engagement. Together with others in silence we have no evidence of their approval, that we are liked and accepted, and we have no way to bolster our fragile sense of identity. We discover the degree to which we define ourselves and evaluate our **inner** sense of worth through the feedback we receive from the words of another. We may feel panic—almost as if starved of air.

Without that constant stream of input, information, and reassurance, we find ourselves feeling anxious, agitated, and uncertain. We are tempted to flee, forgetting that it is not truly possible to flee from ourselves.

Restraining ourselves from flight, we discover that beneath the initial feelings of discomfort or panic that silence evokes there lies the possibility of discovering a new depth of intimacy, **communion**, and peace with the people around us and with ourselves. We learn to release the conclusions, assumptions, and judgments we have previously relied upon to define and describe both others and ourselves. We change, other people change, life changes—from moment to moment.

The images and conclusions solidified through our speech and thought can never fully describe the life of anyone or anything. They describe what we think, assume, or imagine. Refraining from speech allows a new way of **sensing**, seeing, and understanding to unfold. Letting go of our words and all their associations allows a quality of wonder and mystery to emerge. The age-old traditions of seclusion and silent retreat are catalysts of transformation. Our attention becomes naturally

Disturbance, explored

with skillfulness and

dedication, is not negative

or chaotic but the path to

transformation.

Our need for security can imprison us.

085

attuned to ourselves and the ways we engage with life on a moment-to-moment level. Stripped of distraction and preoccupation, we are **visible** to ourselves. Our unexamined conflicts, fears, aspirations, confusion, disappointments, and hopes unfold in wave after wave. Silence removes our familiar ways of hiding from ourself, and we can feel deeply disturbed and unsettled.

We are experiencing the painfulness that signals waking up. Every monk, nun, and mystic who has sought the refuge of silence has undergone this same discomfort. A path to awakening that successfully bypasses the life of our heart and mind is yet to be **discovered**.

The tradition of silence is in a very real way intended to disturb us—to stretch our psychological, emotional, and spiritual horizons. Disturbance, explored with skillfulness and dedication, is not negative or chaotic but the path to transformation. For anything new to be discovered in this life, we need to be willing to let go of the

old. To discover the richness and joy of silence, we are asked to leave the noise behind. To understand what is true in life and in ourselves, we are asked to release the familiar strategies, images, and conclusions that confine us. The way to the ecstasy is through embracing the agony.

Much of our life is dedicated to constructing illusions of safety, certainty, and reliability. We seek to protect ourselves from fear and vulnerability through habit, order, explanation, and the countless strategies we possess to avoid the unfamiliar. We spend massive sums on **security** systems, guards, locks, and walls to protect the fearful mind from the unexpected and unpredictable. We dedicate immeasurable amounts of thought and energy in the same pursuit of safety. We entrap ourselves within the habit of fear. Part of us longs for change, vitality, new horizons, and understanding. Part of us is deeply ambivalent and reluctant and regards change as disrupting and threatening.

In every spiritual journey we will meet moments of difficulty, struggle, and obstacles, just as we meet these moments in our life. We wonder whether all the effort is worth it, feel discouraged by the lack of obvious results, doubt our capacity for inner transformation, or despair at the habitual nature of our minds.

We can spend years trying to create a world of security and safety, ever vigilant against danger, seeing our aspirations wither and the disappointments of our hopes, until finally it dawns on us that it is crucial for us to discover the ways of inner transformation, joy, and the peace of stillness.

overshadowed

Spending time in silence, alone with ourselves, listening to the inner discord and exhaustion born of a life dedicated to busyness, security, and certainty, we come to understand that we cannot always blame the world for the agitation and anxiety we live with. The way we are seeing and being in the world is the root of the confusion and restlessness. We can spend years trying to create a world of security and safety, ever vigilant against danger, seeing our aspirations wither and the **disappointments** of our hopes, until finally it dawns on us that it is crucial for us to discover the ways of inner transformation, joy, and the peace of stillness. Our longing for freedom must finally become more compelling than our longing for certainty. Despite our fear of change, we turn our attention inward to attend to who we are in this moment and welcome the turbulence we encounter.

In every spiritual journey we will meet obstacles, just as we do in our life. We wonder whether all the effort is worth it, feel discouraged by the lack of obvious **results**, doubt our capacity for inner transformation, or despair at the habitual nature of our minds. None of these feelings are strangers to us; they are familiar visitors in our life. The difference is that instead of desperately trying to drown these difficult moments in layers of busyness and distraction, we come to understand that they ask for our attention, mindfulness, and **compassion**.

turn our attention inward to attend to who we are in this moment and welcome the

turbulence we encounter we turn our attention inward to attend to who we are in this

moment and welcome the turbulence we encounter

Silence provokes a quality of existential fear and doubt. Each moment we step into a silent

Genuine peace is discovered in the midst of agitation; true compassion is born in the turmoil of pain; fearlessness is found in our willingness to explore the fears and anxieties that shadow us; and genuine silence emerges from the waves of restlessness we learn to attend to.

Moments of ease, safety, reassurance, and the friends in our lives all serve to soothe and console us.

genuine silence emerges from the waves of restlessness

Our habitual response to moments of difficulty is to endeavor to overcome them, to succumb to them, or to act them out in our actions, choices, and speech. Perhaps we come to understand the lethal consequences of suppression, the exhaustion of willpower, and the sorrow of regret, and realize that in the journey of awakening we must learn new pathways of response and understanding.

Amid the difficulties we meet in our life and heart, we learn the strength and refuge of silence. It is impossible for us to fix every problem, to overcome ourselves, to find a perfect world or an enduring certainty. Genuine peace is discovered in the midst of agitation; true COMPASSION is born in the turmoil of pain; fearlessness is found in our willingness to explore the fears and anxieties that shadow us; and genuine silence emerges from the waves of restlessness we learn to attend to. Moments of ease, safety, reassurance, and the friends in our lives all serve to soothe and console us. Our difficulties, obstacles, and enemies are here to awaken us. They shatter complacency and invite us to learn new ways of seeing and response.

Silence provokes a quality of existential fear and doubt. Each moment we step into a silent space, we leave behind us our familiar strategies, habits, and identities. We face the deep spiritual and existential question of understanding

Our difficulties, obstacles and enemies are here to awaken us. They shatter complacency and invite us to learn new ways of seeing and

088

Life is an amazing landscape in which we make an everexpanding journey of discovery

It is the questions that enliven and inspire us…. Each time we ask the question we are undertaking a journey into the unknown and the unfamiliar. It ceases to be frightening but becomes a journey of transformation and joy

Perhaps we come to understand the lethal consequences of suppression, the exhaustion of willpower, and the sorrow of regret; and realize that in the journey of awakening we must learn new pathways of response and understanding

who we are apart from all that we possess, enact, and perform. The prospect of being "no one" evokes profound anxiety. Descending into silence, we grow increasingly aware of how many of our values, **aspirations**, standards, and judgments we have inherited from others, and we are invited to explore what is authentic and meaningful to us.

What is it that makes our hearts sing? What do we truly long for and value? What does it mean to be free and live an authentic life? Initially we may find ourselves desperately searching for a definitive answer to these questions to solve the anxiety they provoke. We fear that not finding an immediate and absolute answer will leave us floundering in aimlessness, meaninglessness, and confusion. We come to understand at last that it is the questions that are far more significant than the answer. It is the questions that enliven and inspire us. **Staying** close to the questions, making room in our hearts for them, we discover a new openness and intuition. There may never be a right answer that fully satisfies us, no perfect life to live, and no perfect person to become. Each time we ask the question, we are undertaking a journey into the unknown and the **unfamiliar**. It ceases to be frightening but becomes a journey of transformation and joy.

We can learn to accept questions as answer, in themselves and to become open to insight.

Silence is a place of

mystery. We cannot

predict what will emerge

and unfold. Moments of

darkness and sweetness

live in silence; our

demons and our angels

reside there. Learning to

befriend and be intimate

with silence, we probe

that mystery, are startled

into wakefulness, and

understand what it

means to be truly alive,

open, and vital.

Bristlecone pines grow slowly and are among the oldest living things

How often do we travel the well-worn paths of anger, agitation, judgment, fantasy, and anxiety? How often do we travel the well-worn paths of anger, agitation, judgement, fantasy, and anxiety?

Learning to listen fully to the chaos, suffering, and fear that are the daily diet of countless people is the beginning of compassion, empathy, and the motivation to alleviate sorrow.

AWARENESS

habits protect us from change

Silence transforms us. It holds the power to touch and transform all of the events, relationships, and engagements in our life. We discover that silence brings us to a new intimacy, a deeper communion with the people and circumstances we have previously found fraught or overwhelming. Tasting a deeper stillness within our own being, we no longer feel compelled to escape from ourselves into a world of distraction or flee from a life that has previously been experienced as overpowering. Silence teaches us about sensitivity and the richness of being wholeheartedly present. We discover that silence is a powerful refuge, not limited to particular places or times, but a sanctuary that can be invoked in even the most frantic moments and circumstances. Silence teaches us about the possibility of deep calmness and serenity that is not dependent on rejecting the world, but learned through profound steadiness, attentiveness, and poise. Thich Nhat Hanh, a contemporary Vietnamese Buddhist monk, spoke of the perilous journeys refugees undertook at the end of the Vietnam War. In flimsy boats,

Whatever our field of work, we can learn to bring our awareness to focus in it.

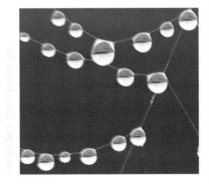

*We cannot choose
whether or not to be
in this world. We
can elect how we
relate to our life.*

with little food or water, and prey to pirates, frightened people set out in search of safety. "If there was just one calm person in the boat," he said, "it would mean the difference between life and death for everyone on board."

Silence teaches us about awareness. For anything at all to change inwardly or outwardly, we must first be aware. It is awareness that enables us to deepen in understanding and **compassion**. Awareness is the mother of empathy, generosity, freedom, and a deeper union with life. It is also the forerunner of creativity, radical transformation, courage, and the capacity to travel new pathways in our heart and life. Awareness awakens us and brings to fulfillment our capacity for deep peace, balance, and wisdom. Awareness teaches us to engage life with a lightness of heart, to attend to the minute details of each moment and discover the richness they offer.

We do not always need to change the circumstances of our lives to find the silence and happiness we seek. It is not yet more thoughts, sensations, experiences, and achievements that will provide the **stillness** and intimacy our hearts long for. We do not always need to change our life to find profound peace; we may well need to change the way in which we live our life. Awareness shows us the possibility of making new beginnings, bringing a heightened sensitivity and care to how we live and altering our relationship to the **inner** and outer events of our life. We cannot choose whether or not to be in this world. We can elect how we relate to our life.

surrendering to habit, we lose touch
with our precious capacity to see anew

The first casualty of awareness is habit. It is a fortunate casualty. Unaware, we live **habitually**, speak habitually, act habitually, respond habitually, and live only on the surface of existence. Habit suffocates vitality, distances us from reality, and armors us against being truly touched by the ever-changing rhythms of our life. Our habits, comfortable and familiar as they may be, bind us to a past that has already gone by, to a world of assumptions and images. Habits serve to protect us from change. Examining our life in the light of awareness we discover how habitual we are not only in our actions and **speech** but also in our thinking. The tired images and **beliefs** about who we are, who other people are, and the nature of life recycle endlessly through our minds. Habits are behaviors and images born of the past to protect us from the present. **Surrendering** to habit, we lose touch with our precious capacity to see anew, to live in harmony with the changes life brings, and to fulfill our capacity to be fully alive, creative, and responsive.

In the light of awareness habit falls away, all of our conclusions and images are shattered, and we learn to see in a way we have never seen before.

Awareness is a deep receptivity and sensitivity of heart we can nurture in all the circumstances and moments of our life. Instead of rushing through a meal, simply satiating your hunger, savor every mouthful. Sense the texture and flavor, see the colors of the food. Experiment with just one task that regularly occurs in your day, how you walk up the stairs in your home or how you pick up the telephone. Instead of hurrying in order to get on with something else, attend to each movement of your leg, the sensation of your foot on the stair, the touch of your hand on the banister. Let the phone ring more than once before you pick it up, then sense the feeling of touching the handset, its touch on your ear, and listen as if to your dearest friend.

Awareness teaches us to let go of what is no longer helpful. Fully present where we are, with what we are doing, we learn to let go of hurrying. There is nothing more important to attend to than the moment we are in. Letting go of hurrying, we find stillness and balance in the moment, rather than eternally leaning forward into the next activity or task. We learn to experience life directly and clearly when our perception is no longer clouded by habits. We let go of resistance as we approach each moment and activity of our day with affection, giving it our wholehearted awareness. Agitation and anxiety are released as we discover that the refuge of stillness is always available to us.

Living in the moment is central to Buddhism.

Awareness makes menial tasks, into meditation.

habits suffocate our capacity to make new beginnings

How often do we travel the well-worn paths of anger, agitation, judgment, fantasy, and anxiety? How often do we travel the well-worn paths of anger, agitation, judgement, fantasy, and anxiety?

Agitation and anxiety are released as we discover that the refuge of stillness is always available to us.

There is

nothing more

important

to attend

to than the

very moment

we are in.

Awareness embraces all things, not just the outer events of our lives but the subtle, quiet movements of our heart and mind. We come to understand that habits suffocate our capacity to make new **beginnings** inwardly. How often do we travel the well-worn paths of anger, agitation, judgment, fantasy, and anxiety? Do we really need to confine ourselves in those often-painful prisons, or can we learn to travel new pathways?

In moments when you feel most beset by habitual patterns of thinking, experiment with bringing a simple, interested awareness to **explore** what you are experiencing. The nature of awareness is that it rejects nothing, embraces all things. We are often so busy trying to get rid of difficult **feelings** that we forget what a difference it makes to greet them with awareness, welcome them, befriend and understand them. The habit of endlessly attempting to divorce ourselves from painful feelings only serves to solidify them and reinforce their truth.

We are often so busy trying to get rid of difficult feelings that we forget what a difference it makes to greet them with awareness, welcome them, befriend and understand them.

Monastic life encourages the discovery of the present.

Learning to be more deeply intimate with silence and stillness in our lives, we emerge with a heightened sensitivity and acute presence that transform everything we touch.

Learning to be still and receptive in some of our most insistent and painful emotional and psychological habits does transform them. We discover that in the light of awareness many of these habits begin to soften. We are less tempted to define or describe ourselves by waves of feeling and begin to see ourselves in a fuller, **deeper** way.

Awareness is essentially a deep, receptive listening that liberates and empowers us. We learn to listen to ourselves, to our emotional and psychological landscape, opening to and receiving the lessons and richness born of the moment. A Jewish mystic once remarked, "Of what avail is the open eye if the heart is blind." Silent, alert listening brings the intimacy and

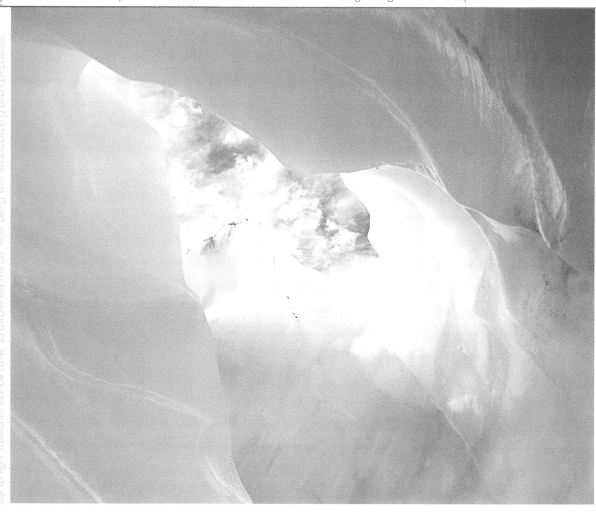

Just as light transforms this ice cave, so awareness fills our inner being with understanding and compassion.

Awareness grows in the grist of our daily life, a path we learn to cultivate and treasure, teaching us the ways of stillness.

Learning to listen fully to the chaos, suffering, and fear that are the daily diet of countless people is the beginning of compassion, empathy, and the motivation to alleviate sorrow.

our world and relationships are saturated with words, yet impoverished in receptivity and listening.

communion we have always sought. We learn to listen to life and all of the people we encounter. Our world and relationships are often saturated with words, yet impoverished in receptivity and listening. In the times of greatest pain and sorrow in our lives, it is the compassionate listening offered by another that heals and strengthens us. It is our capacity to listen that inspires us to reach out and touch the heart of another. Learning to listen fully to the chaos, suffering, and fear that are the daily diet of countless people is the beginning of compassion, empathy, and the motivation to alleviate sorrow.

Awareness is simple; remembering to nurture awareness in every moment of our life is what we struggle with. Each moment we remember to turn toward our present experience, we are deepening and strengthening our capacity for awareness and **wakefulness**. We are learning to be still in the midst of chaos, to be calm in the presence of agitation, to bring serenity to times of anxiety, and to be intimate with all things. Awareness grows in the grist of our daily life, a path we learn to cultivate and treasure, teaching us the ways of stillness. Learning to be more deeply intimate with silence and stillness in our lives, we emerge with a heightened sensitivity and acute presence that transforms everything we touch.

we long for the **future** 104

We forget that it is attention that

reminds us to be still, to listen fully

to the laugh of a child, glory in

the touch of the sun on our face,

and touch the heart of another.

The eternal and immutable truth of everything

in this life is that everything changes.

Learning to let go of what has already gone

by is a path to peace and stillness.

THE INNER EYE

in this life—everything changes

The paths to silence are many

and varied; the sages of the past and present bequeath to us their guidance and wisdom, yet each one of us must learn to travel our own path. The essential message of every great spiritual teacher and tradition is that we must learn to see

through our own eyes and discover our own way to stillness. The indispensable element needed for beginning any spiritual journey is wholehearted, mindful attention. Attention awakens us, illuminates all things, and reveals the silence we seek. The harvest we reap from the seeds of attention are the inner joy, balance, clarity, and compassion we bring to each day of our life.

Every moment of true attention is a moment of wonder. It is **attention** that allows the conclusions and assumptions of the past to fall away, freeing us to see all things anew. Total attention forges a powerful bond of connection between us and our present moment. Deep attentiveness is profound sensitivity; we are touched, moved, and taught by the events, people, sights, and sounds we encounter.

wholehearted attentiveness

There are those who proclaim the miracle of being able to travel to distant planets, to walk on fire. The most wondrous miracles of our lives are actually found in the deep wakefulness and awe discovered in wholehearted attentiveness. Attention is a state of balance and poise in which we are no longer swept away by the force of the inner and outer events of our life. Wholehearted attention is an embodiment of respect and reverence through which we learn to tend to the tiniest details of our lives.

In the busyness of our days it is easy to neglect or dismiss our own capacity for genuine attention. Without attention, we skim over the surface of life, sleepwalk through our days, or find ourselves repeatedly **overwhelmed** by the events we encounter. We forget that it is attention that reminds us to be still, to listen fully to the laugh of a child, glory in the touch of the sun on our face, and touch the heart of another. Our capacity for love, **empathy**, and intimacy is awakened through our willingness to be wholeheartedly present in this life. Alienated from authentic attentiveness, we long for the future, for dramatic life experiences and events that will awaken, enliven, and inspire us. Learning the richness of deep attentiveness, we discover the wonder and richness in the simplest sight, sound, encounter, and feeling.

Attention is the medium that connects us with the changing rhythms of our body, mind, heart, and life. Attention awakens us as we pay closer attention to all the details of our life and we discover that every breath, step,

Our capacity for love, empathy,

and intimacy is awakened through

our willingness to be

wholeheartedly present in this life.

Our life begins with our first breath; our last breath is the ending of our life. Our breath is always with us, our companion in every moment and encounter. Our breath is a refuge of calmness we can return to every moment we become lost in busyness or swept away by the force of events or habit. Remembering to be awake, sensitive, and present within just one breath is a powerful reminder to be awake and connected with our life.

sound, and thought can be a gateway to silence. Each moment that we are fully attentive, we are present in this moment wholeheartedly. The joy, stillness, and depth we yearn for will not emerge from our memories of the past or our hopes for the future, but in the present moment that we enter with sensitivity and wakefulness.

There are myriad ways through which we learn to cultivate clear and wholehearted attention. All of them ask for **dedication**, practice, discipline, and love. One of the simplest ways to learn to be present in our life is to learn to be attentive within our breathing. Our life begins with our first breath; our last breath is the ending of our life. Our breath is always with us, our **companion** in every moment and encounter. Our breath is a refuge of calmness we can return to every moment we become lost in busyness or swept away by events or habit. Remembering to be present within just one breath is a powerful reminder to be awake and **connected** with our life.

The eternal and immutable truth of everything in this life is that it changes. Learning to let go of what has already gone by is a path to peace and stillness. Learning not to hanker over a future that has yet to come is a path to calmness and balance.

As we learn to be more intimate and awake within our breathing we discover that the nature of our breath reflects the nature of life. Our breath is fluid, moving and constantly changing just as all of life reflects change.

learning to be present within our breathing

teaches us to be present in the whole of our life

Experiment with taking just a few moments, several times a day, in which you bring a wholehearted attention to your breathing. Be aware of the beginning of your breath as it touches your upper lip and enters your nostrils. With your **attention**, follow the movement of your breath as it passes through your throat and descends into your chest and abdomen. Notice the point when your inbreath turns to an outbreath, and continue tracing with your attention the full movement of your exhalation. Notice that when we are fully present within our breathing we are present within our body and this moment. As you establish a **mindful** attention within your breathing, let your body soften and relax. Fully present within our breathing, we learn the art of calming our mind and body.

You may notice that after even just a few moments your attention jumps away from your breath into memories, plans, ideas, or daydreams that appear far more enticing or interesting than the simplicity of just breathing. Don't judge, blame, force, or try to control. These are our usual and habitual responses when our life fails to adhere to our plans and expectations. Awareness and sensitivity cannot be measured by the number of consecutive breaths we can count but by the quality of our attention and presence. Learning to be present within our breathing teaches us to be present in the whole of our life, mind, and heart. The moments when your attention departs from your breath are also gateways to depth and stillness. Instead of becoming preoccupied with or lost within the waves of thinking or imagery, simply bring the same **wholehearted** attention to illuminate just what you are experiencing in that moment. Notice if it is planning, comparing, imagining, or remembering that has arisen, just being aware of the essential themes of the mental activity. As attention deepens and we refrain from obsessing about the thoughts and images, they will also fade away in the light of clear attention, and we return to be present within the next breath.

Learning to harmonize our attention within the natural rhythms of our breathing is a lesson in discovering the secret of peace everywhere in our life.

What happens when we try to hold on to a sound that is already passing, cling to a meal that is already ended, or try to make the person we love stand still for us?

Rain is part of the eternal cycle keeping the world alive

We cultivate mindfulness within breathing not to escape from our lives but to **illuminate** them. Learning to be clearly present within just one breath at a time is part of our learning to be equally present in one event, one conversation, one experience, and one thought at a time. We learn to cultivate mindfulness of breathing not to subdue or reject the life of our minds and hearts but to discover a calm stillness within it. In the most frantic and confused moments of our day, we can always come back to the simplicity of mindful breathing. We remember to pause, to be still and present.

As we learn to be more intimate and awake within our breathing, we discover that the nature of our breath reflects the nature of life. Our breath is fluid, moving, and constantly changing, just as all of life reflects change. Nothing we can see, touch, feel, or experience is immune to the process of change. The sounds we hear, the **sensations** we experience, the people we love, and our own images of ourselves—none of these things are constant, lasting, or eternal. What would happen if we **endeavored** to prevent an inbreath from changing into an outbreath? We would set ourselves apart from the nature of our bodies and gasp for life. Learning to harmonize our attention within the natural rhythms of our breathing is a lesson in discovering the secret of peace everywhere in our life. What happens when we try to hold on to a **sound** that is already passing, cling to a meal that is already ended, or try to make the person we love stand still for us? The result is an inner tension born of trying to grasp that which is already passing and to set ourselves apart from the reality of this **moment**. The eternal and immutable truth of everything in this life is that it changes. By living in the present moment, we are acknowledging and accepting this fundamental truth. Learning to let go of what has already gone by is a path to peace and stillness. Learning not to hanker over a future that has yet to come is a path to calmness and balance.

Being present within our breathing, we learn to bring a simple, calm attentiveness to the thoughts, feelings, and sensations that constantly arise and pass. Greeting them with gentle, kind attention, we understand that they are not obstacles to silence but powerful reminders to listen deeply, let go and be fully here in this moment and this life. Silence does not depend upon subduing our mind, abandoning our heart, or divorcing the world. Silence is born of learning to calm the waves of unease born of preoccupation, obsession, agitation, and anxiety. Attention, being wholeheartedly present with one breath, one sound, one sight, one event at a time, teaches us the path of calmness and stillness. We come to understand that learning to let go in this life is one of the most powerful gateways to silence.

The richness of attention can be cultivated in countless ways and circumstances. We can dedicate times in our day to learning how to listen deeply. We assume we know how to listen, yet as we deepen in sensitivity we become increasingly aware of how often our listening is interrupted by the flow of concepts, judgments, and evaluations that flood our consciousness. How fully do we ever listen to the sound of a bird, a passing train, a siren in the night, or the person in front of us? Do any of these **sounds** truly disturb stillness, or does the disturbance come in the wake of the prejudices, judgments, resistance, or concepts with which we laden those sounds? When we take the time to sit in silence, we can experiment with staying connected to the sounds that arise until they fade away, rather than being lost in our stories and reactions to them. We learn to retract our prejudices, and so to look and listen once again.

How often do we truly listen to ourselves? Sitting in silence, turning our attention inward, we begin to attend to the many voices that flow through our mind. We hear the voice of the critic, the wounded child, the controller, the planner, the dreamer, and the quieter voices of our heart. We learn to listen to the tones of our thoughts and feelings without blame or prejudice, and they soften and calm in the light of gentle, clear attentiveness.

As our capacity to listen deepens, we also begin to sense the gaps between the sounds, thoughts, and images that at first appear so incessant. Within those gaps we hear the sound of silence. Addicted to busyness, we often perceive the gaps between events as blank spaces waiting to be filled with some new pursuit. Learning to be at home in silence, we probe the richness and depth offered in those gaps. We may be surprised to discover that in the gaps between events we hear our hearts sing and discover joy and authentic peace. True joy, we come to understand, is born not of the successes, possessions and achievements of our life, but of our capacity to rest in silence and know a deep inner sense of completeness.

The deeper we delve into silence, the clearer the world appears to us

Although spiritual traditions can guide us, we must make our way into silence.

In learning to calm and still our inner turbulence it is not the object of attention, the breath or sound that is of primary significance, but the inner focus, clarity and wholeheartedness of connectedness that we learn to cultivate.

The journey of silence does not require esoteric, exotic, or special rituals, initiations, or spiritual paraphernalia. We do not achieve, possess, or accumulate silence. It is immanent in all things and all moments, awaiting our discovery. Attention is a means of letting go of the inner clutter and discord that cloud the stillness of the moment.

In learning to calm and still our inner turbulence, it is not the object of attention, the breath, or sound that is of primary significance, but the inner focus, clarity, and wholeheartedness of connectedness that we learn to cultivate. Some people find it helpful to experiment with simple visualization practices. Place before you a leaf from a tree, a simple picture, a stone, or an evocative image, and allow your gaze to rest gently on it. Explore it fully with your attention, noticing the subtle colors and shades and all of its details. Close your eyes and see if you can recall the image in your consciousness. After a few moments it may slip away; just open your eyes to visually connect with the object once more. As you calm and settle in greater stillness, you may discover that you are able to hold the image in your inner attention for longer periods of time. Attention is a process of integrating energy. By learning to bring wholehearted focus to anything in our life, we are learning to cultivate a communion in all moments.

The journey of silence does not require esoteric rituals. We do not achieve, possess, or accumulate silence. It is immanent in all things and all moments, awaiting our discovery. Taking time to be still in your days, you will find it enough just to close your eyes and turn your attention to the life of your body. Sense the different feelings and sensations that appear and fade away through your body. Notice the sensations born of the contact of your body with the chair or floor, the feeling of your clothing on your skin, the sound of your pulse and heartbeat. Let your body relax into stillness, refraining from trying to fix or alter anything. Attending to your body, you may begin to notice how your body is a repository for many of the emotions that have been difficult to acknowledge consciously. Feelings of anxiety, tension, resistance, fear, and anger become stored in our bodies, impairing our well-being. Attending to those places of contraction and tightness with a gentle, calm attention allows them to unlock and soften.

"For a sincere student, every day is a fortunate day."

Allow your body to speak to you, and sense the way in which your body reflects the life of all bodies. The pain and pleasure, birth and death, beginnings and endings, youth and aging, sickness and health we sense in the life of our own body is a reflection of a universal story. Listening to our body, we learn not to struggle with this story but to make peace with our life. We learn that modification, manipulation, denial, and judgment serve only to agitate our heart and alienate us from life. The lessons of acceptance, compassion, kindness, and sensitivity learned through attending to our bodies are life lessons that bring us ever closer to stillness and peace.

We all hold within us a powerful, often untapped, capacity for both sensitivity and mindful attention. As we explore our potential to be fully present, one moment at a time, we discover a growing vitality, appreciation, and energy beginning to emerge. In the Zen tradition of Buddhism there is an adage that says, "For a sincere student, every day is a fortunate day." The moments of dedicated silence we cultivate in our days begin to spill over into all the events and circumstances of our lives. Like waking up from a dream, we find ourselves at times startled and surprised by the beauty and depth of everyday realities.

We begin to understand that for us to be deeply touched, taught, ar ved by our life, we need to be wholeheartedly present within it.

We begin to understand that for us to be deeply

touched, taught, and moved by our life, we need

to be wholeheartedly present within it.

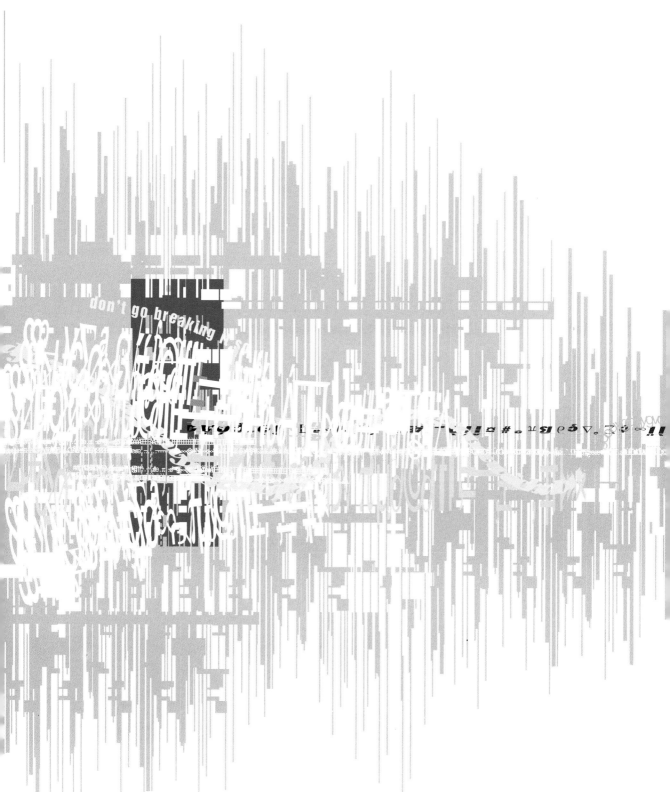

3

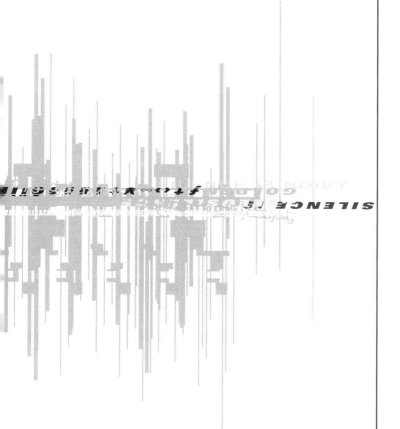

nothing in this world is **permanent**

or static or stands **still**

All that we believe ourselves to be in

this moment is a result of everything we

have absorbed, experienced, and

come to accept as a truth.

We all depend on one another—to live, to love, to be nourished, and to create a world that is free from conflict.

---

start to live the life you wish to live

"Know thyself" is the perennial

instruction of every great spiritual tradition. To live our life in an authentic way, we need to understand ourselves deeply. The journey within is the foundation of every other journey we will make in our lives. There is no more worthy task in this life than to understand ourselves fully and deeply. Self-understanding is the basis of all peace, creativity, and capacity to live with

The journey of self-discovery uncovers incredible treasures.

others in a fearless and compassionate way. The great Chinese sage Lao-tzu advised, "To know another is to be wise. To understand oneself is to be enlightened."

Culturally, we invest vast amounts of time and resources in the pursuit of knowledge, yet we invest so little in the search for self-understanding. Knowledge we can gain and accumulate. The primary prerequisite for self-understanding is silence and the capacity to listen deeply to all the changing facets of our being.

Desperate to find an answer to the question "Who am I?" we try to define ourselves through accomplishment, success, accolades, analysis, and performance. We are rarely **satisfied** with the definitions that rest upon such fragile foundations.

Our pursuit of knowledge and prestige can actually limit our horizons.

We appreciate that none of these transient gains can provide us with enduring happiness, freedom, authenticity, or a true understanding of how to live in a sacred way. Silence invites a different order of understanding, a deeper intuition that speaks to us of a way of knowing ourselves that is not dependent upon all we have gained and accumulated. As Lao-tzu said, "In the pursuit of knowledge, every day something is gained. In the pursuit of understanding, every day something is let go of."

An intriguing exercise in self-understanding would be to set yourself the task of writing your autobiography in just two short verses. Begin each sentence with the words "I am...," and then proceed to describe yourself at this moment in your life as fully as possible. We might be tempted to describe ourselves by listing details such as our gender, status, relationships, culture, race, and appearance. Our autobiography might include details of our personality and our fears and hopes.

we understand there is a d

between understanding our

"What does it matter if we can travel to the moon if we cannot cross the abyss that separates us from ourselves? This is the most important of all journeys. Without it, all of the rest are useless."

become

someone

special

nothing in this world

is permanent

or static or stands still

we change, our understanding of who we are is constantly

being altered by new information and new experience

Rereading our autobiography, we might discover how much it reflects the opinions, feedback, values, and standards of the various authorities and people that influence us. The autobiography we write today is no doubt quite different from the one we would have written ten years ago or the one we would write ten years in the future. We **change**; our understanding of who we are is constantly being altered by new information and new experience. It is hard to find a sense of ourselves that is constant and enduring, independent of the changing conditions and circumstances of our life.

Just as nothing in this world is permanent or **static** or stands still, we, too, are in an ongoing process of being reborn and changed. Only our definitions, conclusions, and images are static. They have little to do with the vitality and shifting rhythm of living. Rereading our autobiography, we understand there is a difference between understanding ourselves and knowing what we think about ourselves. Facing the reality that no definition,

accomplishment, accolade, or role can ever suffice to describe the vastness and **fullness** of our being can be a startling, even frightening discovery. Probing the facade of our autobiography, we begin to sense the ways in which our list of definitions may even serve to create a veneer of certainty and identity that protects us from a deeper and more rewarding self-understanding. Thomas Merton, the Christian visionary, wrote, "What does it matter if we can travel to the moon if we cannot cross the abyss that separates us from ourselves? This is the most important of all journeys. Without it, all of the rest are useless."

Culturally, socially, and professionally we are exhorted to excel, be someone special, succeed, and make our mark upon the world. The pressure of expectations, goals, and milestones to achieve accompanies us from our early childhood. The **rewards** we are promised are status, prestige, acceptance, admiration, and even love.

All of us want to live **meaningful** and creative lives, yet too quickly assume that the fulfillment we long for will result only from our success in being someone "**special**" and adopting the ambitiousness and busyness that the attainment of our goals seems to entail. Rather than attaining the inner happiness and creative life our hearts yearn for, we may discover that we have ended up living a life of self-promotion rather than **self-expression**. Prestige, admiration, and praise fail to fill the vacuum of inner loneliness or meaninglessness; nor do they bring us the happiness and peace born of self-understanding.

a strong sense of identity and individuality

In the pursuit of this esteemed individuality we may also isolate ourselves from a true sense of community with others or communion with life.

Psychologically and culturally we are encouraged to develop and pursue a strong sense of **identity** and individuality. The ability to take care of ourselves, follow our dreams, and not be a victim in life is assumed to rest upon our capacity to develop a powerful sense of "self." In the pursuit of this esteemed individuality we may also isolate ourselves from a true sense of community with others or communion with life. We find ourselves competing to be more attractive, successful, and **worthy**, and turn potential companions and allies into enemies or intruders.

We endeavor to solidify our sense of individuality through the trophies of our achievements, plaudits gained, and the evidence of our successes. Yet by the same means we solidify our fear of loss, failure, and rejection, and our deepening sense of isolation.

The experience of isolation and inner alienation translates into a fearful life in which we are ever vigilant against signs of danger, failure, judgment, and rejection.

We find ourselves competing to be more attractive, successful, and worthy, and turn potential companions and allies into enemies or intruders

In a study of happiness undertaken by a Harvard professor, it was concluded that the happiest people are those who are least self-conscious.

We forget that any identity or sense of self that relies upon what we have gained or gathered is always fragile, subject to change and dissolution.

A sense of community is what ties our sense of point.

It is essentially a busy and fraught life, dedicated to protecting all that we have gained, bolstering our defenses, and **eternally** trying to convince ourselves that we are indeed loveable and worthy. "Good," "bad," "right," "wrong," "acceptable," and "unacceptable" become the commandments by which we live, guiding our choices and actions. We forget that any identity or sense of **self** that relies upon what we have gained or gathered is always fragile, subject to change and dissolution.

In a study of happiness undertaken by a Harvard professor, it was concluded that the **happiest** people are those who are least self-conscious. The capacity to step out of the cycle of inner judgment and assessment is to lay down a burden of fear and agitation. When we are less willing to define ourselves by any image or role, we are less **impacted** by the judgments, rejections, or blame of another. Self-consciousness is perpetuated by the voice of the anxious inner critic that craves acceptance, admiration, and affirmation above all else.

If I hope to climb a mountain or remain where you are and face yourself?

Self-consciousness is perpetuated by the voice of the anxious inner critic that craves acceptance, admiration, and affirmation above all else.

presence

In a spiritual journey dedicated to wisdom, silence, and freedom, we learn to surrender self-consciousness and devote ourselves to being conscious of the whole phenomenon of self, separation, and isolation.

We can be supremely happy sitting on a crowded train, cleaning out our attic, or preparing a meal. It is not the result or the destination that delivers the happiness but the experience of being wholeheartedly present and aware in that moment. The quality of our presence in this world continually determines our experience of it. If we are always intent on goals, destinations, or achievements we rarely offer ourselves the opportunity to be present in anything at all. We are spurred on by our desire to be admired and be productive. Silence is profoundly forgiving and accepting. It contains no judgments or comparisons. It offers a release from self-consciousness and all of the tension born of our uncertainty of ever being "good enough" or "worthy enough."

We can be supremely happy

sitting on a crowded train,

cleaning out our attic, or

preparing a meal. It is not the

result or the destination that

delivers the happiness but the

experience of being

wholeheartedly present in that

moment. The quality of our

presence in this world continually

determines our experience of it.

Silence is profoundly

forgiving and accepting. It contains no

measurement, judgments

or comparisons. It offers a

release from self-

consciousness and all of

the tension born of our

uncertainty of ever being

"good enough" or

"worthy enough."

If we base our happiness on future events, we will never actually arrive at happiness.

How can we know

all of who we are

unless we take the time

to be silently with

ourselves, and to listen

to the many voices

of our heart?

As long as we are desperately clinging to our more shallow definitions, we cannot heed the quieter whispers of our heart that speak to us of new horizons and new ways of seeing and expression. In silence, we broaden our horizons.

Beneath the facade of the stern and ambitious executive, there hides a man who wants to scale mountains or cradle an infant.

The fear, often unconscious, that keeps us on the treadmill of striving, busyness, and performance is that without all of this activity we will degenerate into a life of invisibility, worthlessness, and inertia. Until we begin to befriend silence and everything it reveals to us, we rarely question this equation. Silence teaches us about inner abundance. We learn we are more than just a competitor, a role, or a definition. In truth we are a tapestry of multi-colored threads—emotions, aspirations, dreams, and longings—that are interwoven and constantly changing. Beneath the veneer of the efficient professional, there may lurk a wild-eyed woman who longs to walk barefoot in the grass in spring. Beneath the facade of the stern and ambitious executive, there hides a man who wants to scale mountains or cradle an infant. By hanging onto external labels, we limit rather than add to our "worth." As long as we cling to shallow definitions, we cannot heed the quieter whispers of our heart that speak of new horizons and new ways of seeing and expression.

How can we know all of who we are unless we take the time to be silently with ourselves, and listen to the many voices of our heart? Silence reveals to us what really sustains and nurtures us in this life, the dreams we need to follow, the aspirations we need to fulfill and the joy that is possible for us. From this priceless understanding, we can start to live the life we wish to live and not the life prescribed for us by fear or expectation.

We understand that a worthy life can never be defined by dramatic achievements, stunning attainments, or anything we possess. A worthy life is a life that leaves a legacy of compassion, care, sensitivity, and peace. A creative life cannot be measured by the trophies we've gathered or the goals we've achieved but by the way in which we treasure every gesture, every step, and every choice. A meaningful life may be the one in which we are deeply dedicated to expressing the gifts we have for

Silence teaches us about inner abundance. We learn we are more than just a competitor, a role, or a definition. In truth we are a tapestry of multicolored threads—emotions, aspirations, dreams, and longings—that are interwoven and constantly changing.

It is not possible to alter, recover, or change the experiences of the past, just as it is not possible to guarantee or control the future.

We are part of the dazzling complexity of the world.

135

intimacy, peace, and sensitivity rather than in promoting any image or identity. A wise Indian teacher told his students, "Wisdom teaches me I am nothing, love teaches me I am everything." We discover the great freedom in being "**no one special.**" We can be responsive to the inner and outer changes of our life, we can play, care, be active, and be still. We can be as fluid as a mountain stream yet at the same time steady, poised, and clear. We also discover the illusion of isolation, and the way that it is sustained by our own fears and an absence of self-understanding.

We are intimately connected with one another and with all of life. We are constantly being affected by the changes taking place in our world and in turn impact the world with each of our gestures, choices, and thoughts. We all depend on one another—to live, to love, to be nourished, and to **create** a world that is free from conflict. Separation is not a realistic option for any

of us. We carry within us everyone that has ever loved us, hated us, and taught us. On a cellular level, we carry all of the experiences of our lives—the fears and joys, the sorrows and delights, the peaceful and the challenging. All that we believe ourselves to be in this moment is a result of everything we have absorbed, experienced, and come to accept as a truth. The person we become in future **moments** is born of what we experience, believe, and accept as truth in this moment. It is not possible to alter, recover, or change the experiences of the past, just as it is not possible to guarantee or control the future.

Deeply understanding ourselves in the present offers us very real choices about the kind of future we will live. Transformation can occur only in the moment we are awake and present. Self-knowledge is a state in which we are deeply intimate with every aspect of our being. Listening inwardly, we attend to the facets of ourselves that we appreciate and respect, and therefore allow these qualities to find expression in our lives.

Our capacities for generosity, empathy, and commitment are honored and celebrated. The search for self-understanding may also reveal aspects of ourselves that we fear and would rather disown or deny. Our capacity for anger, greed, jealousy, and anxiety will also emerge in the light of unconditional inner attention. These, too, ask to be welcomed, accepted, and understood. Self-knowledge asks us not to abandon any part of ourselves, not to neglect or ignore any inner quality—but to bring a kind, gentle attentiveness to all.

To Martin Luther King Jr., accolades were unimportant next to living a committed life

We do not need to find an answer to the question "Who am I?" Any answer will fall short of the truth of who we are and will be a denial of the reality that we are constantly changing. The willingness to apply the question to all the descriptions we hold about ourselves is a way of probing their reality. We discover that few of our assumptions are an absolute truth.

We do not need to find an answer to the question "Who am I?" Any answer will fall short of the truth of who we are and will be a denial of the reality that we are constantly changing. The willingness to apply the question to all the descriptions we hold about ourselves is a way of probing their reality. We discover that few of our assumptions are an absolute truth. We learn in the light of the question "Who am I?" to dive beneath all of the conclusions and descriptions and descend into a deeper, receptive silence. Here we can listen to what truly nurtures and sustains us, what our deepest values are, and the most profound longings of our heart. A life that is born of stillness, inner attunement, and receptivity is an authentic life. Shortly before his death, Martin Luther King, Jr., gave a speech in which he asked not to be remembered for all the accolades that had been showered on him. He asked to be remembered as having lived a committed life, living for peace, justice, and dignity. Self-knowledge shows us the way to a committed and authentic life.

peace is born of our **profound**

commitment to being at **peace**

Peace begins in our willingness to embrace the difficult and challenging, whether inwardly or outwardly. It is learned in just one moment at a time. Peace is discovered in each moment we commit ourselves to no longer being a cause of harm.

The challenges that come to us we no longer perceive as threats to flee from, but as invitations to learn the lessons of peacemaking.

INNER PEACE

we catch glimpses of genuine peace

As human beings we long for peace. Every day of our lives a war is being waged somewhere in the world, communities destroyed, and lives shattered. The terrible conflicts that continue to devastate our world we see reflected in a microcosmic way in our own hearts, minds, and relationships. We struggle with our adversaries, live in fear of our enemies, compete with our colleagues, and disdain and reject aspects of our own minds and hearts. A life without peace is a painful, agitated, and fearful life. To deepen as human beings and to live with integrity and compassion, we need to discover the source of peace within our own hearts.

Throughout our lives we catch glimpses of genuine peace. They are moments of deep warmth, trust, and intimacy. At times, these moments catch us by surprise, and we wonder how they were born. We find ourselves alone in nature, **sharing** a meal with a good friend, or simply waking one morning and touching a tangible sense of stillness. We are not struggling with anything or anyone inwardly or outwardly, and we suddenly realize that where we are and who we are in

A common fear is that a life without chance would be boring and desolate.

this moment is enough. No sense of anything missing haunts us. These are the moments in our lives that make our hearts sing with joy and wonder. Yet they seem almost accidental. They are not born of heroic struggle, they are not delivered to us by anyone else, and they are not reliant upon perfection in our lives.

We tend to project peace into the future, to be found after we have gained the perfect partner, job, and lifestyle. We tend to think of peace as something that awaits us after we have achieved the ambitions that preoccupy us. We sometimes believe that peace is the reward for a lifetime of struggle. We may even believe that peace relies upon our eradicating from our lives everything and everyone that disturbs, challenges, or unsettles us.

Peace projected into the future, divorced from the daily grist of our lives, is a peace that is rarely encountered in the present. Genuine peace is to be discovered in all of the activities of our lives and in every moment. Peace is immanent. If we truly treasure peace, each of us is asked to turn toward the reality of our lives and ask ourselves what would be needed to be at peace in this moment. What is needed to release the struggles, wars, and tension in our own hearts? What, in this moment, is truly lacking? All of us sense the damage inflicted upon the world and upon ourselves through conflict and struggle. We all appreciate the urgency of living in the spirit of peace and embodying it in all the moments of our lives. Yet there can also be an inner ambivalence in our relationship to peace. As much as we yearn to shed the pain and alienation of conflict, we also discover the addiction we have to intensity, drama, excitement, and the roller coaster of highs and lows that seem to offer vitality, interest, and passion to our lives.

We may suffer during times of intensity and drama, yet these experiences also serve to awaken us and make us feel alive. We may fear that peace would bring with it a bland, indifferent, and uninspiring life. It is not always easy to acknowledge that our pursuit of intensity and drama reveals an inner vacuum of richness and vitality that we are fleeing from. In moments when we step back from the pursuit of intensity and the extremes of experience and sensation, we can begin to sense an inner numbness that disturbs us deeply. Underlying that numbness we also sense the loneliness, fears of unworthiness, regret, and boredom that we are desperately trying to escape. The habit of self-abandonment can come to govern our lives, and we discover that it is easier to find intensity than to discover peace.

The price of peace is the willingness to be still and present within ourselves. To calm our own heart and unlearn the habit of self-abandonment is the beginning of the process. We cannot be at peace with anything or contribute to a peaceful world unless we understand what it means to calm our own troubled hearts. Opening to our struggles with a generous heart and facing our life just as it is are the first and last steps in spiritual practice.

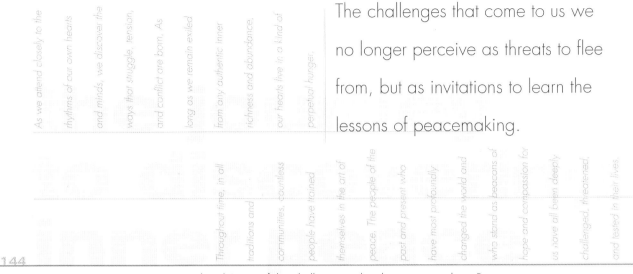

The challenges that come to us we no longer perceive as threats to flee from, but as invitations to learn the lessons of peacemaking.

Peace is not the absence of the challenging, disturbing, or unsettling. Peace is born of our heartfelt willingness to greet the encounters and experiences of our inner and outer world, without prejudice, resistance, or fear. We learn to live in a way in which we have no enemies to struggle with and no battles to win. The challenges that come to us we no longer perceive as threats to flee from, but as invitations to learn the lessons of peacemaking.

Throughout time, in all traditions and communities, countless people have trained themselves in the art of peace. The people of the past and present who have most profoundly changed the world and who stand as beacons of hope and compassion for us have all been deeply challenged, threatened, and tested in their lives. Martin Luther King, Jr., Mahatma Gandhi, the Dalai Lama, Julian of Norwich, and Mother Teresa, to mention just a few of the mystics and dissidents of our world, have all been asked to understand the nature of peace and freedom. They have educated themselves in the universities of bigotry, tragedy, and terror. Their classrooms have been in slums

We prowl the world of experiences, sensations, achievements, and possessions, trying to satiate a hunger that can never be satisfied. The truth is that as long as we are not at peace with ourselves or connected with inner joy, we can never gain, achieve, or possess enough to appease this relentless hunger. We find ourselves obsessing about what we don't have and struggling to get rid of what we have. We no longer want, or we lose interest in, what we gain. We are conditioned to always want more—more fame, sex, status, possessions, and accolades—believing that this is the path to happiness and the end of searching

and prison cells, in the midst of oppression and deprivation. Each one of them has without doubt been asked to make a deep inner journey to understand the causes of war and peace. If we treasure and long for peace, we too are asked to make this journey and to learn from the university of our lives. We discover that peace is not a destination to be reached but a way of living, relating, speaking, and being.

As we attend closely to the rhythms of our own hearts and mind, we discover the ways that struggle, tension, and conflict are born. As long as we remain exiled from any authentic inner richness and abundance, our hearts live in a kind of perpetual hunger. We prowl the world of experiences, sensations, achievements, and possessions, trying to satiate a hunger that can never be satisfied. The truth is that as long as we are not at peace with ourselves or connected with inner joy, we can never gain, achieve, or possess enough to appease this relentless hunger. We find ourselves obsessing about what we don't have and struggling to get rid of what we have. We no longer want, or we lose interest in, what we gain. We are conditioned to always want more—more fame, sex, status, possessions, and accolades—believing that this is the path to happiness and the end of searching.

We undertake the inner journey of seeking for the source of contentment, happiness, and peace.

It is a powerful realization as we come to understand that in the busyness of our search for something the world of objects and experiences can never provide, we have simply forgotten how to live.

Time and experience teach us the essential lesson that trying to satisfy the "never-satisfied" mind does not result in peace or happiness. Instead, the result is the tension of trying to defend the things that we obtain to make ourselves feel better, the fear of loss, and the sorrow of becoming increasingly alienated from ourselves. The more we gain or achieve, the more that elusive peace seems to slip farther into the future. We continue to try to convince ourselves that happiness lies just around the next corner; when we get the right job or the right partner, or move to the right area. Eventually, the disturbing truth dawns on us: we will never be able to gain or possess enough to satisfy a heart that is deeply conditioned to scour the external world in the search for happiness and peace. It is a powerful realization as we come to understand that in the busyness of our search for something the world of objects and experiences can never provide, we have simply forgotten how to live. All of our assumptions and goals need to be scrutinized in the light of this new perspective.

However beautiful, dazzling, or exciting the experience or place, lasting happiness can be found only within us.

For many of us this is a startling revelation which, leads us to explore a voluntary simplicity in our lives. It is not a rejection of, or withdrawal from, the world, but more a quality of spiritual curiosity. At this point we undertake the inner journey of seeking the source of contentment, happiness, and peace.

For many of us this is a startling revelation, which leads us to explore a voluntary simplicity in our lives. It is not a rejection of, or withdrawal from, the world, but more a quality of spiritual curiosity. At this point we undertake the inner journey of seeking the source of contentment, happiness, and peace.

Each moment of our lives begins the seed of inner peace

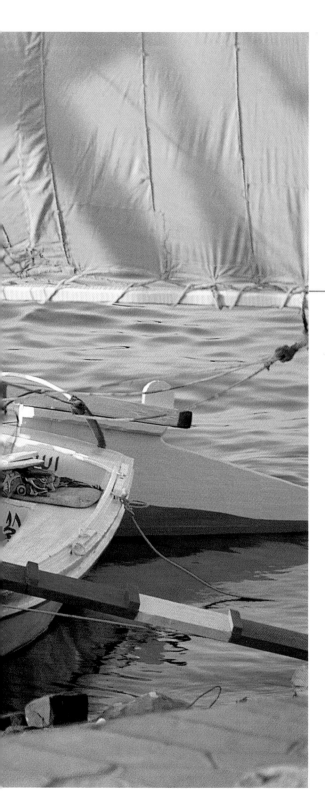

As we step back a little from the intensity of our expectations and demands on life, we may be startled to discover that every moment in our life holds everything that is needed to discover deep peace and contentment. As we nurture a little more space and openness in our lives, we perceive not a dreaded inner vacuum of impoverishment but an alert, responsive heart with immense capacity for appreciation, sensitivity, and understanding. As we are less compelled by addictions to busyness, intensity, and acquisitiveness, we discover the simple and profound joy of living wholeheartedly, listening to the world, and living with inner richness.

Peace begins in our willingness to

embrace the difficult and challenging

whether inwardly or outwardly. It is

learned in just one moment at a time.

Peace is discovered in each moment we

commit ourselves to no longer being a

cause of harm. Peace is born of our

profound commitment to being at peace.

Endless conflict, war, and struggle are born of the territorial nature of our own minds, which create borders between nations, individuals, and communities. Fear leads us to want to possess, own, cling to, and grasp tenaciously all the things we call "mine." "My" country, race, gender, opinions, religion, and class live in a perpetual tension with all that is seen as different and separate. Conflict is a clash of "I" and "you," "mine" and "yours."

There is nothing that has the power to create more division, prejudice, and hatred in this world than the tendency to shelter within the confines of the borders created within our own minds. Generosity, tolerance, acceptance, and understanding are sacrificed upon the hateful altars of possessiveness and clinging. Paradoxically, we pursue beliefs, opinions, creeds, and possessions as a way of ensuring our safety and security in this life, yet what they bring in their wake is in fact insecurity, division, and fear.

Peace in our hearts and in our world is born of our inner willingness to discover a greater generosity, tolerance, and understanding. The enemy we struggle with is ourselves in a different form, sharing with us the longing for happiness, respect, and understanding.

Our enemy is created out of our fear. In the service of peace we learn to approach our enemies and come to understand that, like us, they share the capacity to be hurt and to suffer, and the yearning to be free from pain. We learn to probe our prejudices and judgments, to dive beneath our stereotypes and images, understanding that peace in our world demands that each one of us learns to let go of the borders in our heart that divide us.

Our enemies are not always external. Inner peace is shattered by the intensity of judgment, disdain, and rejection we perpetuate within our own psyche. Self-hatred and self-denial can be deeply ingrained habits that continue to convince us of inadequacy and

Peace begins in our willingness to embrace the difficult

Instead of consenting to judgment, disdain, or dismissal, we learn to soften, open, and listen deeply.

To find peace in this world, look for it in your heart first.

worthlessness. We make an enemy of aspects of our own being—our bodies, our personalities, our minds, our emotions. How can we ever expect to find peace in our lives if we do not know how to be at peace with ourselves? The art of peacemaking asks us to learn new pathways within our hearts.

We need to rediscover our own capacity for loving-kindness, gentleness, compassion, and sensitivity. We are not helpless before the force of our psychological and emotional habits, no matter how long a history they carry. Instead of consenting to judgment, disdain, or dismissal, we learn to soften, open, and listen deeply. Peace begins in our willingness to embrace the difficult and challenging, whether inwardly or outwardly. It is learned in just one moment at a time. Peace is discovered in each moment we commit ourselves to no longer being a cause of harm. Peace is born of our profound commitment to being at peace.

who is my **enemy**

who is my **friend**

willingness

compassion

The refuge and sustenance we long for are born of silence, self-understanding, and the inner strength possible for all of us.

In finding the strength to surrender our inclination to avoid our lives, we discover the capacity to embrace the reality of living without flinching. We simply do not have the power to solve all of life's dilemmas and difficulties.

INNER STRENGTH

there is not always a solution

The strongest people in the world are not those who can move mountains, vanquish their enemies, or control their destinies. The strongest people in the world are those who can love unconditionally, live with deep integrity, and find compassion in the midst of hardship and pain. It takes immense strength to stand with steadiness amidst the storms of our life, to face fearlessly the moments when our certainties appear to disintegrate and to meet the 1,001 moments of sorrow our lives will bring.

Wise teachers throughout all times and traditions have encouraged us to understand what it means "to be a light unto ourselves." There is an urgent need for us to be awake in our lives and discover this quality of inner strength and empowerment. Our world, planet, communities, and societies are in a process of serial catastrophes that produce immense suffering and alienation. This world does not need more despair, anger, or opinions. Our planet, communities, and families will be healed by the courage, integrity, compassion, and strength of individual people who stand as beacons of dignity, wisdom, and freedom.

Whatever our work of life, we will need strength to face sorrow and pain.

Rarely does it occur to us that stillness, receptivity, and silence may offer to us the healing, ease, and strength that will lead us out of confusion and sorrow.

We tend to regard moments of discomfort, challenge, and uncertainty as bad news; they may instead be the doors to transformation and stillness we have always sought.

The refuge and sustenance we long for are born of silence, self-understanding, and the inner strength possible for all of us.

Each one of us will experience moments in our lives when our world seems to fall apart. People we have relied on may disappoint us; we are separated through death or change from those we love; our dreams are surrendered in the face of more demanding realities; our bodies become sick and age. Elements of our lives that we thought were permanent and on which we had based our happiness suddenly vanish. We face the countless moments of disillusionment, failure, regret, and insecurity that come to us in this life. In these moments of uncertainty, chaos, and pain the presence of friends and loved ones can comfort us, support us, and sustain us. We learn, though, that they do not have the power to deliver us from life with all its uncertainties and sorrows. In these moments we are asked to find the inner strength and balance to embrace the reality of our lives without flinching. We are asked to find the inner wisdom, stillness, and compassion that will rescue us from the clouds of confusion and fear threatening to overwhelm us. In the midst of confusion and anxiety, where can we go that will offer a true refuge? What can we rely upon to sustain us? The refuge and sustenance we long for are born of silence, self-understanding, and the inner strength possible for all of us.

We tend to regard moments of discomfort, challenge, and uncertainty as bad news; they may instead be the doors to transformation and stillness we have always sought. In these moments we encounter our familiar patterns and strategies of pushing away the difficult, heroically trying to avoid the unpleasant, or blaming the world or ourselves for our misfortune. We see our chronic inclination to find solace in explanations and solutions and our desperate endeavors to "fix" the problem. Instead of finding the ease and peace we long for, we spiral into further agitation and confusion. Rarely does it occur to us that stillness, receptivity, and silence may offer to us the healing, ease, and strength that will lead us out of confusion and sorrow.

The truth is that we live in an uncertain world that provides few guarantees. We cannot "fix" every moment of difficulty or discomfort; there is not always a solution to the pain of living; and we may not always be able to relieve all suffering. Our efforts to find an easy solution can in themselves lead to more suffering. Ceasing to regard discomfort and sorrow as a problem, we take a major step in the journey of discovering inner strength and stillness. We come to understand that to transform sorrow we must first accept it as a natural part of life—rather than reacting as if we had caught a rare disease.

The events and experiences we may feel most inclined to avoid may turn out to be the most direct pathways to inner **transformation**. Finding the strength to surrender our inclination to avoid our lives, we discover the capacity to embrace the reality of living without flinching. We simply do not have the power to solve all of life's dilemmas and difficulties. By embracing life and accepting it as it comes, we can find the **power** to stay present and connected, and to deepen in understanding. It is a process that takes great courage to embark upon, especially if we have unconsciously devised means of avoiding reality—such as compulsive behaviors around work, relationships, substances, and distraction.

Don Juan, a wise teacher in the Shamanic tradition, remarked upon the difference between a warrior and an ordinary person. He taught that to an ordinary person every event is seen as either a blessing or a curse, whereas to a warrior everything is a challenge and an invitation to new understanding. Surrendering our inclination to avoid or suppress the difficult moments in our life, we also surrender our deep fear of being overwhelmed, consumed, or battered by those events. Avoidance serves to fan the sparks of fear until they turn into towering infernos, beyond anything that the reality of the situation warrants. By the very act of facing reality with an open, calm mind, we divest events and people of much of their power to terrify us. In directly facing the events and circumstances that most frighten us, we allow ourselves to see them clearly and observe that they are not quite so towering as we had assumed.

We learn to bring the strength of silence to the most chaotic moments in our lives and discover a new way of being in their presence. When we no longer feel compelled to push hurt away, we can use it to develop a deeper sensitivity and compassion. When we no longer reject disappointment, we understand what it has to teach us about forgiveness and tolerance. When we no longer hide from change, we liberate ourselves to live fully.

Mahatma Gandhi and his followers used silence as a way of facing up to their own inner demons of rage, fear, and confusion. They learned to find a strength and balance with which nothing in their inner landscape could overwhelm or terrify them. They did not seek to suppress fear, but understood that true fearlessness lay in the willingness to meet and embrace fear without hesitation. The inner strength derived from profound openness and receptivity became the outer strength that they were empowered to bring to their quest for justice, dignity, and freedom. Surrendering our own reluctance to experience our inner demons, we discover that there is little in the world that can terrify us. We find that we can turn to all the joys and sorrows, the disappointments and losses that come to us without being overwhelmed or lost.

It takes immense strength to live in a compassionate way in a world that is so burdened with pain, violence, rage, and sorrow. Endless images in the media remind us of the deprivation, terror, starvation, and abuse that afflict countless people in our world. The people begging on our street corners, the bullied children in our schools, and the disenfranchised in our communities are all part of our lives and make an impact on our hearts. To sense the pain of so many lives is almost unbearable. At other times we do all that we can to distance ourselves from the distress or busy ourselves with blame and explanation.

Compassion is not weakness. It takes remarkable strength to live with an open and receptive heart and to let the waves of sorrow wash through us. It is not indifference that leads us to turn away from pain but the fear of helplessness and powerlessness. A homeless beggar on a San Francisco street corner confided that the greatest sorrow of his life was not the absence of possessions, family or home, but the recurrent experience of being invisible and disconnected. Days would go by, he said, when not one single person who passed him by would be willing to look into his eyes. To live in a sacred way we all need to feel connected and acknowledge our interdependence with other human beings—our friends and family, those we work with, and humanity as a whole. Instead of simply assuaging our conscience by handing a few coins to the homeless person, we might reflect that given different circumstances and conditions we could be where he is and he could have our life. In the light of this, we might ask ourselves what warmth and acknowledgment we may be able to offer.

Compassion is a deep, heartfelt care for every single life in our world. It empowers us to move out of the inertia of fear and powerlessness to live in a way that is actively dedicated to ending pain, division, and conflict. Compassion does not demand grand or heroic gestures but the willingness to turn toward pain rather than flee from it, to face difficult situations rather than pretend that they are not happening.

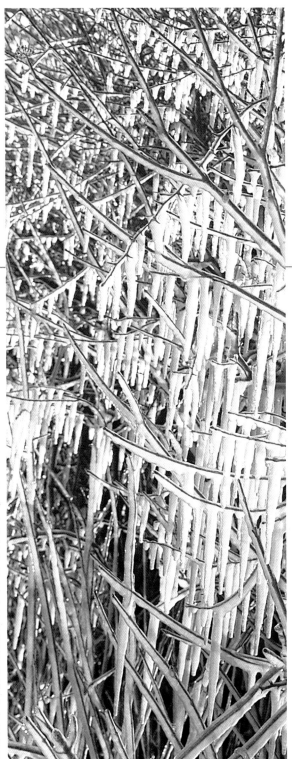

Just as winter is part of the life cycle of the earth, so suffering has a value in our lives.

Life will continue to present us with countless moments and encounters that ask for deeper and deeper levels of compassion. It is easier to hate than to love, to harbor resentment than to forgive, and to protect ourselves rather than **opening** to life. Learning to be steady, poised, and still within ourselves, we discover that it is possible for each of us to embody a living compassion in our thoughts, speech, and actions. Compassion is not just an intention, but an active way of engaging with the world.

It takes great strength to live consistently with integrity, honesty, and dignity. We are so often tempted into pathways of living and acting that compromise our integrity and leave behind them harmful residues of regret and guilt. These, in turn, can trigger further compromising behavior. It is easier to participate in gossip in order to feel as if we belong in a group than to remember the harm we may be inflicting upon the individual being disparaged. How often we are tempted to exaggerate or deceive another in order to protect or **promote** ourselves. It can be deeply challenging to live a committed, ethical life in the midst of a widespread cultural ethos that covertly encourages us to serve our personal interests and comfort before anything or anyone else.

Dedicating ourselves to not harming anyone or anything on our planet through our actions, words, or thoughts requires immense strength. Committing ourselves to speaking honestly and truthfully, to respecting the dignity of everyone around us, and to living in a clear and conscious way asks for deep inner courage. We may not be showered with rewards and praise for the integrity we embody, but we will live with a peaceful heart and a calm mind.

To forgive those who have threatened, harmed, or hurt us, in the past or in the present, asks for a profound inner **strength**. In the face of injustice, threat, or hurt it is easier to retaliate and perpetuate cycles of anger and fear than it is to forgive those who have harmed us and to understand their behavior. An elderly Tibetan monk who had spent years in harsh prisons, where he was regularly beaten and tortured, emerged to speak of the forgiveness he cultivated as a daily practice toward those who wronged him. The act of forgiveness does not condone violence, injustice, or oppression. Instead, it is the refusal to assume the role of the avenger or hater in our own heart. It is a true defiance of the power of the oppressor.

It takes both great strength and profound understanding to refrain from the avenues of rage, blame, and violence that arise in the times we feel most deeply hurt or violated. We can learn to translate the inner anger we inevitably experience in the face of injustice and oppression into **creative** and productive means of response and action that cannot be ignored. In this way the ancient cycles of hatred and violence can be broken, and we can move forward in a new direction.

When the world around us seems broken, we need inner strength to sustain us.

Love is deeper than self-

gratification, romantic

images, or intense

passion. Love is the

willingness to stay

connected with another.

To live in a way in which we

feel beset by opponents and

enemies is to live defensively

and with great agitation.

There will be moments

when we falter or lose

our way. Increasingly we

discover the strength to

begin again, to renew

our connection with

the moment we are in.

"Who is my enemy? My mind is my enemy.

Who is my friend? My mind is my friend."

It takes immense strength to love unconditionally. It is not difficult to love those who please, flatter, and admire us. It is deeply challenging to bring warmth, care, and **acceptance** to those who challenge, contradict, or displease us. To live in a way in which we feel beset by opponents and enemies is to live defensively and with great agitation. The Buddha once said, "Who is my enemy? My mind is my enemy. Who is my friend? My mind is my friend." Our enemies are solidified through the waves of resentment and fear that well within us when we are hurt, disappointed, or judged. Lost in those waves, we separate and distance ourselves from another person. Separation is not neutral; it is a **space** that fills with agitation, blame, and anger, and creates only sorrow.

Love is deeper than self-gratification, romantic images, or intense **passion**. Love is the willingness to stay connected with another. It takes immense strength not to falter in our loving, when we feel it is not returned or when another person fails to met our expectations and needs. We can understand love as our willingness to be generous, tolerant, understanding, and **forgiving**. Love is embodied in our willingness to see beneath the changing moods, actions, and stories of another person and to acknowledge that we share with him a deep longing to be cared for, accepted, and seen in the fullness of our being. Love is not for cowards or for those who are reluctant to walk through the fires of misunderstanding, distance, and fear. To love just one person in this world, wholeheartedly and without conditions, asks for immense commitment.

To undertake any worthy journey in this life, whether it is climbing a mountain or descending into silence, asks for perseverance, dedication, effort, and love. There will be moments when we falter or lose our way. Increasingly we discover the inspiration to begin again, to renew our **connection** with the moment we are in. This is the strength that is asked of us if we are to discover the richness of silence.

In the midst of our troubles, we can find strength and calm.

we make peace with **everything**

A compassionate heart knows how to listen

deeply, to see beneath the surface appearances

and stories that divide us from one another, and is

dedicated to the end of sorrow and division.

So much of the conflict, division, struggle, and pain in our world is unnecessary, born of fear, alienation, and the territorial mind.

SERENITY

silence is vast and without boundaries

The mystics, sages, and great social activists of past and present do not linger eternally in their cloisters and caves. Their greatness lies in their willingness to engage wholeheartedly with life, to transform injustice, oppression, and sorrow. Genuine inner transformation is measured by the compassion, dedication, and sensitivity we bring to each action, choice, and moment we engage with.

Buddhism teaches that spirituality is not divorced from day-to-day living.

Silence, stillness, and even the most profound insight would be of limited value if they were confined within the walls of a monastery or reliant upon our total and eternal withdrawal from life. It is not idealism, fine words, or even good intentions that transform our world, but the impact of each one of us living a life truly committed to honesty, compassion, and **dignity**

In the Zen tradition of Buddhism it is often said that if you want to truly know a Zen master, ask their spouse. Our actions and behavior speak louder than a thousand words, our words reveal the state of our mind and heart, our busyness reveals our anxieties and unease. By learning the richness of silence, and receiving the wisdom it reveals, we learn not only to approach our inner world with care and

Compassion is a simple but powerful tool for good in the world

sensitivity but equally to approach our life in a new way. The greatest teachers are not those who have transcended the world around them, but those who have transcended fear, hatred, and greed.

In silence we learn how alienation, sorrow, and division are created and perpetuated in our own hearts and minds. Listening inwardly we experience directly the damage we do to ourselves through judgment, blame, denial and obsession. In silence we learn some of the most significant lessons of our lives; what harms us and what heals us. Learning to befriend ourselves in silence, we discover that acceptance, tolerance, generosity, and learning how to let go restore us, renew us and reconnect us with serenity, peace, and happiness.

The lessons we learn in the territory of our own hearts and minds are life lessons that apply to every living being. They are not merely intellectual bubbles that have no use in the real world. So much of the conflict, division, struggle, and pain in our world is unnecessary, born of fear, alienation, and the territorial mind. Our world, our communities, our families and ourselves cry out for healing. There is no greater gift that we could offer to ourselves or to another than the gift of compassion. A compassionate heart knows how to listen deeply, to see beneath the surface appearances that we sometimes accept as true reality and beneath the stories that divide us from one another. All of us share the capacity to feel and to be aware. Grief, fear, sorrow, confusion, anger, and hurt observe no boundaries. No being is exempt from the need for the compassion of their fellow beings. We are all, invariably, enriched by the loving and caring presence of another.

We all share a longing for love, happiness, intimacy, and acceptance. We all flourish in the presence of trust, tolerance, kindness, and compassion. Our capacity to be aware brings with it new possibilities of deep understanding and transformation. In bringing a

We discover a new serenity within ourselves when we are no longer driven by fear or denial.

At times, we all need to find the compassion within us to say no to the causes of pain, to withdraw our consent from the creation of division and harm, and to honor the dignity and integrity of everyone in our world. Compassion teaches us how to bring to an end the perpetuation of alienation and pain without ever rejecting the perpetrators.

compassionate attention to the shadows and storms of our own hearts we soften and calm them. We discover a new serenity when we are no longer driven by fear or denial.

Silence is vast and without boundaries. From silence emerges compassion—the capacity to meet and embrace all our storms without prejudice or judgment. Compassion is a spiritual strength that changes the world within and around us. We all know what it feels like to be filled with anger, resentment, and blame. Equally, we know what it feels like to love, to accept, to befriend, and to be **intimate**. Experience is the great teacher, inviting us to dedicate ourselves to understanding and kindness.

Compassion is a profound inner commitment to the well-being, dignity, integrity, and freedom of every living being in our world. True compassion does not thrive on sentimental or romantic ideals. Compassion has the flavor of great kindness but is rooted in a commitment to end division, sorrow, and conflict. There are times when genuine compassion is expressed in a forthright and **resolute** way.

For each of us a commitment to end conflict must carry with it a heartfelt refusal to accept or condone the unacceptable. We come to learn that prejudice, bigotry, injustice, exploitation, and oppression are unacceptable simply because they perpetuate sorrow, pain, and division. In this light, we can see that it can take great courage to live a truly compassionate life.

At times, we all need to find the compassion and courage within us to say no to the causes of pain, to withdraw our consent from the creation of division and harm, and to honor the dignity and **integrity** of everyone in our world. This may put us at odds with the pervading culture of the day. Just as compassion teaches us how to bring to an end the perpetuation of alienation and pain, it also instructs us not to reject the perpetrators.

172

We do not always have to

travel the pathways of

alienation and pain.

Forgiveness, generosity, and

kindness are possible for each

of us. We can all learn to

cease being a cause of harm

and to understand what it

means to be a cause of peace.

Making peace with ourselves, we make peace with everything in our lives.

We find that life continues to present us with countless moments and events that ask us to respond with profound compassion. To change the world is too big an ambition—to respond to our world of this moment with compassion is possible for each one of us. How do we approach the homeless vagrant on the street, the colleague who disturbs us, the neighbor we resent, and the people who have harmed us? The distant siren in the night, the images of tragedy flashed on our television screens, and the moments of inner despair we encounter all invite us to discover the power of compassion, to open our hearts and to listen deeply to the experience of our fellow beings. Compassion is not a future destination or romantic dream. In silence we encounter the rage, hurt, resentment, and prejudice that live in our own hearts. Learning to open, receive, and explore these most painful places in ourselves, we begin to discover what is meant by genuine compassion. We do not always have to travel the pathways of alienation and pain. Forgiveness,

generosity and kindness are possible for each of us. We can all learn to cease being a cause of harm and to understand what it means to be a cause of peace

Mahatma Gandhi advised that we must be the change we wish to see in the world. Instead of regarding serenity, peace, kindness, and compassion as states to be achieved or destinations to arrive at, we can learn to embody them as pathways we commit ourselves to in every dimension of our lives. Serenity and peace in the world must begin with ourselves. They do not rely on our eradicating all the storms and disturbances from our lives but on learning to greet them as allies rather than opponents. Serenity is born when we no longer experience ourselves living in a world peopled by enemies. Making peace with ourselves, we make peace with everything in our lives. Discovering calmness within ourselves, we seek to cultivate it in every interaction and event we engage in.

In silence we encounter

the rage, hurt, resentment,

and prejudice that live

in our own hearts

Serenity and peace in the world must begin with ourselves. They do not rely on our eradicating all the storms and disturbances from our lives but on learning to greet them as allies rather than opponents. Serenity is born when we no longer experience ourselves living in a world peopled by enemies.

Young Buddhist novices learn that serenity is not a state of being but a way of being

Our culture tends to romanticize love, dream of love, and search relentlessly for love. We might wonder why, in our collective search for love, it continues to be so elusive.

In stillness we begin to learn to bring

a loving attention to ourselves.

acceptance and forgiveness

Serenity asks us to love where we are, who we are, and those who are right before us.

Bringing absolute attention to this moment awakens a sense of reverence and sensitivity. We learn to see, listen, touch, speak, and act in a loving way. Everything in this world, inwardly and outwardly, comes alive in the light of unmixed attention.

Our ideals of love are often projected into the future, to be discovered in the perfect soul mate, the ideal family, and the life we have yet to find. Serenity asks us to love where we are, who we are, and those who are right before us. Serenity is not the result of redecorating our lives or relentlessly seeking perfection but of learning to surrender our judgments, prejudices, and fears.

Serenity has its roots in our willingness to approach the simple reality of our lives with wholehearted attention. Love may be both simpler and deeper than the intoxicating allure of passion and desire. Bringing absolute attention to this moment awakens a sense of reverence and profound sensitivity. We learn to see, listen, touch, speak, and act in a loving way. Everything in this world, inwardly and outwardly, comes alive in the light of unmixed attention. It is when we bring loving attention to even the most inconsequential events in our life that we truly start to live.

Loving attention bonds us with the moment, nourishes connection and heals division. The Buddha taught, "Hatred will never be healed by hatred. Hatred will be healed by love alone. This is the eternal law."

In stillness we begin to learn to bring a loving attention to ourselves. It is an attention of healing, acceptance, and forgiveness. It is also an attention of celebration. We learn to honor and rejoice in our growing capacity for trust, wisdom, and compassion.

We also learn to forsake pathways of division. We discover the deep serenity and power of loving-kindness. Love teaches us to cross the boundaries between "self" and "other." The lessons of healing we have learned in our inner landscape become the guiding principles in all of our relationships. We discover that when we forsake self-preservation, self-protection, and self-gratification we undergo a truly heroic transformation of consciousness. The storms of our lives calm before a deepening serenity.

Loving-kindness teaches us the richness of generosity and service. Martin Luther King, Jr. advised, "An individual has not started living until he can rise above the narrow confines of individualistic concerns to the broader concerns of all humanity." We all have the capacity to bring calm to turmoil, kindness to alienation, and serenity to chaos.

Silence reveals to us an inner abundance of richness, sensitivity, and freedom. In the midst of unhappiness and feelings of inner deprivation we grow increasingly closed and defensive. Genuine happiness expresses itself in generosity, concern, and a heartfelt caring for the well-being of all those around us. The transformations that take place within us through silence are reflected in the way that we interact with our world.

Generosity does not demand that we renounce our homes and possessions or impoverish and mortify ourselves. It asks us to recognize that a truly impoverished life is one that is dedicated solely to self-preservation and gratification. Generosity does not demand us to perform grand acts of heroism or self-denial. It does ask us to recognize the essential interdependence of all life. We come to understand that in caring for the well-being of those around us, we care for ourselves. When we selflessly give of our time, attention, and care, our hearts fill with blessings. Richness in our lives cannot be measured by what we have gained externally, but by the quality of our relationships and how we have served all life.

Serenity is the home of those who have forsaken conflict, fear, and hatred. Serenity is the abode of those who live with integrity, dignity, and respect. Serenity is the flavor of inner freedom. The discovery of serenity is as close to us as our next breath, the next step we take with wholehearted attention, and the next sound we receive with deep sensitivity.

...serenity is the home of those who live with integrity, dignity, respect. Serenity is the abode of those who have forsaken conflict, fear, and hatred. Serenity is the flavor of inner freedom. The discovery of serenity is as close to us as our next breath, the next step we take with wholehearted attention, and the next sound we receive with deep sensitivity. We do not need to search the corners of the earth for the remarkable serenity and stillness that await our discovery in this moment. Being still, being present, listening wholeheartedly, we discern

We do not need to search the corners of the earth or explore esoteric religions for the remarkable serenity and stillness that await our discovery in this very moment. Being still, being present, listening wholeheartedly, we discern the heart of serenity.

Our ways of interacting, thinking, seeing, and living

may be radically altered. When our lives and hearts

are no longer consumed by frantic haste,

distractedness, or agitation, they take on a new shape.

So much energy, time, and attention are consumed in trying to avoid, fix, or eradicate the experiences we dislike and fear. An equal measure of time and energy is focused upon trying to find, secure, and possess the experiences we like and want.

---

silence teaches us to live with wonder

Silence is the mother of deep understanding. The mirror of silence reflects all the dynamics of inner life and our ways of relating to the world around us. We are changed by the insights and openings that silence offers to us. Our ways of interacting, thinking, seeing, and living may be radically altered. When our lives and hearts are no longer consumed by frantic haste, distractedness or agitation

they take on a new shape. We are learning to live in a freer and more authentic way. Silence teaches us to live with wonder, thankfulness, and appreciation.

We begin to discover that when we live with deep sensitivity, rather than habit, we approach our lives with curiosity, commitment, and a willingness to learn. A quality of innocence enters our lives in our willingness to see anew in each moment. We find ourselves continually surprised by the daily invitations to let go of fear, find stillness, and live compassionately. Profound freedom and happiness in this life do not rely upon our endlessly changing the scenery of our life but upon learning to live with an open heart and a still mind.

The winds of change continually sweep through our lives. Praise and blame, gain and loss, success and failure, pain and pleasure, beginnings and endings are the extremes of experience that appear to hold the power to exile us from silence and agitate us deeply. So much energy, time, and attention are consumed in trying to avoid, fix or eradicate the experiences we dislike and fear. An equal measure of time and energy is focused upon trying to find, secure, and possess the experiences we like and want. It is a vicious circle that can be hard to break out of. Remaining in the cycle of pursuit and avoidance is a recipe for deep unhappiness, restlessness, and unease.

We love to be praised, to win, to succeed, and to be flattered—they are experiences that make us feel good, worthy, and accepted. While these experiences can all be positive in themselves, the relentless pursuit of them can lead us to unhappiness. Blame, failure, loss, and pain impact deeply in our hearts,

awakening familiar echoes of unworthiness, inadequacy, and low self-esteem. Hooked into the cycle of pursuit and avoidance we find ourselves subject to endless mood swings and changing images of ourselves which are governed by the ever-shifting experiences and circumstances of our lives. In this state, inner stability is at the whim of external events.

The desperate endeavor to control the events of our lives sentences us to fear and agitation. Letting go of our addiction to control brings calm and freedom. When you sit in silence and your worries and projects start to jostle for attention in your mind, do not try to ignore them or shut them away. Let them come and then let them go again. They come and go from our minds, just as they come and go from our lives. Changing events and circumstances are an inevitable reality of life, not to be exaggerated into terrible dramas that we build flimsy walls of avoidance to hide from. Silence helps us to face reality calmly, in perspective, and without fear. We find that we can unlearn fear.

fear of change

Silence teaches us a new way of being with change. It is not only the circumstances of our lives that are in a constant state of flux, but also our emotional reactions to them.

Silence allows us to approach and understand this subjective reality and reveals to us a way of being in which we are no longer governed or oppressed by the changing circumstances we meet. We learn that the silence nurtured within us need not evaporate at the first sign of trouble

Silence teaches us to greet changing circumstances and events in a new way. We discover within ourselves a quality of consciousness and a steadiness of heart that are not shattered by the winds of change in our lives. The pain and fear we habitually experience in the face of change are not inherent in the gains and losses, praise and blame, or pleasure and pain that life brings to us and that we cannot always control. We carry within ourselves a subjective world that is constantly interpreting the events of our lives.

Silence allows us to approach and understand this subjective reality and reveals to us a way of being in which we are no longer governed or oppressed by the changing circumstances we meet.

We learn that the silence nurtured within us need not evaporate at the first sign of trouble. On the contrary, it can be relied upon in just such moments of strife to guide us and help us to cope with the experience. While we must be accepting of external events, we need not grant them the power to make us miserable and fearful.

Change is threatening to us only as long as we demand permanence as a condition for our personal happiness. Loss, failure, pain, and blame have the power to shatter us only in the absence of any genuine self-understanding and inner richness. We get lost in the agitation of pursuing the fixes of fame, pleasure, praise, success, and indulgence only when our sense of self feels fragile and uncertain.

Silence teaches us a new way of being with change. It is not only the circumstances of our lives that are in a constant state of flux, but also our emotional reactions to them. A critical word received from another triggers a spiral of despondency, and we find ourselves lost in aversion and self-blame, convinced of our inadequacy. Hours later we are praised by someone else, our spirits lift, and the world looks wonderful once more. On this roller coaster of mood swings and emotional extremes there is little true happiness. It is through silence that we learn how to step off the roller coaster.

Silence shows us a way of being present within the extremes and changes in a more fearless, curious, and dispassionate way. We learn to receive, accept, and be open to the variety of experiences that life brings us. We learn to probe some of the habitual and historical reactions that are triggered by external events rather than consciously chosen.

Above all, we learn to let go in the midst of change. There is a simple logic to this approach. If we are not so attached to success, we are also not so deeply shattered by

186

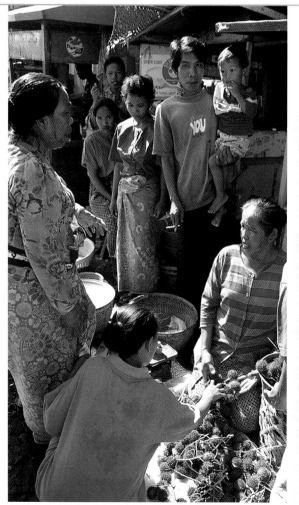

failure. No matter how dramatic, intense, or convincing our experience of this moment is, it is already in the process of changing into something else. If we learn to be more fearless in the face of pain, we are also not driven to pursue pleasure and avoid difficulty. If we learn to be more steady and questioning amid the criticism and blame we will inevitably meet, we will not go through our lives begging for praise. Silence reveals to us an inner authenticity that is profound and free, in which we are less tempted to define ourselves by the changing events of our lives or the changing mood swings of our minds. We learn to live with ease and openness.

Learning to let go in this life is not a path to misery or deprivation, but a path of happiness. It does not sentence us to be "out of control." Discovering a deep inner joy, wholeness, and freedom radically alters our relationship to the world of people, experience, and objects. There will never be enough

gained that can soothe a discontented heart. There will never be enough distraction, busyness, or experience to satisfy a troubled mind. Whatever the discontented person gains, they will always have to face the same mind at the end of the day telling them that they need more. What kind of relationship would we have with this world if we ceased to see it as a solution to inner unhappiness? The joy of silence teaches us to be more generous, caring, and sensitive. When we are established in inner happiness we liberate the people and events in our lives from the tyranny of our demands and expectations. We find ourselves more deeply accepting of the people in our lives.

Expectation is a masterful saboteur of happiness and stillness. We have so many blueprints and maps that we expect life to conform to, so many standards we expect the people in our lives to adhere to, and so many demands on ourselves. Insecure within ourselves, we rely, for peace of mind, upon our our expectations being fulfilled in order to ensure our own desire for safety and certainty. Whether it's what the weather will be like on the weekend or how someone we meet reacts to us, we base our happiness on future events over which we have no control. In silence, we begin to see what a fragile and shortsighted philosophy we have built for ourselves. Eventually, we have to ask ourselves how much disappointment, disillusionment, and despair enters our lives precisely because of our attachment to and dependence on our expectations. We can learn to let go of much of this.

People change, we change, events aren't totally predictable, and they cannot and will not always turn out the way we hoped. This basic reality of life does not have to shatter us and automatically sentence us to an existence filled with frustration, anger, and despondency.

Harmony in this life is born of being attuned to the way things are and not the way we want them to be. This is one of the deepest and most transforming lessons that silence can teach us.

Expectations mask the richness available in reality.

Surrendering our catalog of expectations is not a surrender of vision, aspiration, or direction. It is a surrender of tension. Letting go of many of our demands and expectations, we release the poison of so many of the conditions for loving that tarnish our relationships, both inner and outer.

We come to understand that the gap between "what is" and what we **believe** "should be" is in fact an ocean of sorrow. Although we cannot avoid loss, change, or disappointment in our lives, despondency and despair are optional. Living and relating without conditions and demands changes the texture of all of our relationships.

We find ourselves more sensitive, forgiving, and tolerant. We can love more fully and see more deeply into the heart of another person. We can be more forgiving and tolerant of ourselves; the times we stumble and lose our way are no longer seen as disasters but as invitations to learn and deepen in understanding. We cannot live tomorrow's life today; the only moment we can transform is the moment we are in, and we are no longer so willing to live in hope of some elusive future happiness and freedom. We begin to be intimate with the deep sensitivity, compassion, creativity, and meaning that are born of silence and find ourselves more reluctant to squander our time and energy in the pursuit of transient achievements and distractions.

We live in a fragile world and a fragile body that need care and commitment. We do not know the moment of our death, what the future will bring, or even what the next moment holds. But we are not merely a victim of our past or of the circumstances in our lives. We have the capacity to be still, to awaken, and to live a life that embodies a deep understanding of our inter-connectedness. A recent survey revealed that of all of the people polled, only 2% said that they would wish to be remembered as a person of wealth and success, whereas 85% said they wished to be remembered as a person of goodness and kindness who had contributed in a meaningful way to the world.

Silence reminds us of the power of intimacy, compassion, love, and generosity. We remember that each one us impacts on our immediate world with our actions, speech, and thought. We are participants in the creation of the kind of world we live in and share. Understanding this, we come to make wiser choices about how we dedicate our time, energy, and attention. Expectation and avoidance cloud the fact that perhaps there is nothing more worthy of our attention than a commitment to living just this one moment fully, to listening to the person before us wholeheartedly, and to taking just one step with total awareness.

One of the greatest gifts of silence is the gift of vision. Silence opens many doors of possibility and awakens a deeper sense of aspiration. Our fears often make us feel powerless and helpless and result in the desperate desire always to protect ourselves. The houses of safety we construct to defend ourselves from the dangers of life are too often houses without windows that also blind us to the possibilities of our own hearts and consciousness.

We hear the eternal messages that each one of us has the potential to be awake, free, and a whole human being. Yet our faith in those messages is corroded by life experiences of hurt that have scarred our faith in ourselves. Mahatma Gandhi taught that fear leads us "to lose the way of our spirit." Fear born of the past surfaces in the present, leading us to isolate ourselves from life and to close our own hearts. We become so entangled in worrying about all of the threatening dangers lurking in life that we forget to live. Oscar Wilde, the poet and playwright, wrote "The most terrible things in my life never actually happened."

Silence teaches us to meet our fears, to distinguish between what is past and what is actually present. We discover that all of the thoughts, images, and "what ifs" generated by our fears are far more dangerous and threatening than the object of fear itself. When we learn to be more gentle, curious, and spacious around our fears, many of the barriers and walls we have so carefully constructed begin to dissolve. Learning to trust more deeply in our capacity to be present and open to ourselves, we learn to meet our lives in a more trusting and open way. We realize that in some ways we have become attached to fear, as it serves to stop us from having to deal with the feelings of emptiness within us. We begin to have more faith and confidence in ourselves, and our sense of what is possible for us in this life expands.

The eternal teaching of all great spiritual traditions reminds us to reach for what is possible for each of us. Greatness of heart, rich silence, wholeness,

greatness of heart, rich silence, wholeness,

and joy are the essence of an awakened life.

Vision and confidence teach us never to despair, to give us, or to accept a way of being and living that is less than that which is possible for us.

and joy are the essence of an awakened life. Vision and confidence teach us never to despair, to give up, or to accept a way of being and living that is less than that which is possible for us. It is sometimes wise to be dissatisfied with the presence of discontent, restlessness, anxiety, and alienation in our lives. We are not fated to endure these, and they are not life sentences. We do not need to judge them as signs of inadequacy. We can greet them as messengers that remind us that there is another way of being and living. When we view them in this way, we are less likely to try to suppress or deny these symptoms of unhappiness.

Just one moment, one encounter with deep inner silence speaks to us of the possibilities available to each of us to live a wise, compassionate, and rich life. We come to realize that it is a life that begins in the moment we fully and deeply connect with it, a life of meaning and abundance.

don't go breaking

4

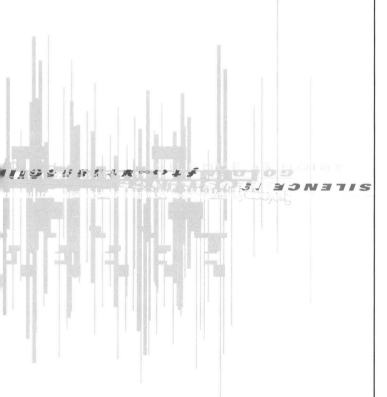

discover seams of spiritual **richness**

seek greatness of heart and **mind**
196

The poetry of enlightenment we have inherited over

centuries sparks a sacred hunger in our own hearts.

On a cellular level we yearn to explore the

possibilities of freedom and communion open to us.

We sense within

ourselves that there is

more to life than just what

we perceive through our

senses and mind.

JOURNEY'S END

the paths to awakening are rich and varied

Spiritual history is a record of men's and women's journeys into the unknown in search of realization and awakening. Mystics throughout time have answered an intuitive call to discover oneness, reality, and enlightenment. The language in which they recount their stories differs, yet we sense beneath the semantic variations a message of timelessness and freedom. We sense within ourselves

that there is more to life than just what we perceive through our senses and mind. We too are drawn, again and again, to discover an inner seam of **spiritual** richness that will bring meaning to life. We long to live in a sacred way and seek greatness of heart and mind. The poetry of enlightenment we have inherited over centuries sparks a sacred hunger in our own hearts. On a cellular level we yearn to explore the possibilities of freedom and communion open to us.

Throughout time human beings have struggled with the tension of the deep desire for safety and the equally powerful wish to discover a greater sense of mystery and **wonder**. We find ourselves caught between these polarities in every decision we make

about our future. Insecurity and anxiety lead us to enclose ourselves in a world of familiarity, predictability, and certainty. Intuition and the voice of the inner mystic call us to travel into unknown territory, to embrace uncertainty, and to explore the horizons of our consciousness. Fear guides us to dedicate immense energy and activity to creating a personal world we can inhabit without being disturbed or challenged. We fill that world with habit, opinion, belief, identity, and assumption to protect ourselves from unwelcome disturbance. At the same time we sense that any genuine spiritual journey must begin with the willingness to have all of our boundaries and assumptions examined and disturbed. Reading the journals of spiritual journeys, we sense the common theme within them: the crossing of all boundaries and confines.

In the Middle Ages sailors hugged the shorelines because they lacked proper navigation instruments to explore the unknown regions of the sea. We

are tempted to confine ourselves within the world of opinions, shared assumptions, and beliefs to avoid falling into the unknown. The first sailor who found the courage to sail his boat toward the distant horizon was moved by faith, curiosity, and the unwillingness to accept limitation. One of our deepest longings is to be undisturbed, yet it seems that awakening is linked to our willingness to be unsettled and seek out new horizons.

Mystics throughout time have made a similar journey of discovery to probe beyond the limits of what they have come to know and understand. The same faith, curiosity, and courage that sustain the intrepid sailor are integral to this inner journey. The true revolutionaries of our time are those who are willing to make the journey into the unknown. The willingness to stretch emotional, psychological, and spiritual horizons, to be disturbed and challenged, are the prerequisites to deep spiritual awakening. We will not get far by clinging to what we know. We will not take ourselves intact into enlightenment.

We travel into uncharted territories of consciousness that are the home of mystery and wonder.

As our commitment to our path deepens, it absorbs our whole being, and we enter into new realms of consciousness. In all spiritual paths we encounter a "fasting" of the mind as a way to nourish the spirit.

The paths to awakening are rich and varied. Service, prayer, meditation, and devotion are just a few of the primary paths undertaken in the quest for awakening. There are those who seek to awaken through withdrawing from the world of busyness, to immerse themselves in a life of contemplation and silence. There are also those who immerse themselves in the world in search of the same awakening. Entering Mother Teresa's home for the dying in Calcutta, you encounter young nuns who learn to see in the faces and bodies of the damaged, desperately ill, and dying the face of Christ. There are people who seek awakening through cultivating altered states of consciousness or experiences of oneness, or through ecstatic states of communion and transcendence. There are also people who seek the sacred in the care of the poor, the imprisoned, and the disenfranchised. One man spoke of his life caring for his severely disabled child as a spiritual quest that asked him to find new depths of patience and love every day of his life.

The shared theme in all of these journeys is one of commitment and dedication. Immersing ourselves in spiritual disciplines or service is a way of dying to ourselves. As our commitment to our path deepens, it absorbs our whole being, and we enter into new realms of consciousness. In all spiritual paths we encounter a "fasting" of the mind as a way to nourish the spirit.

Awakening asks for a profound willingness to let go. Set aside first are the preoccupations and activities of our lives generated by anxiety. We learn to let go of discursive thinking, comparisons, and expectations. We learn to let go of restlessness, fear, and desire for certainty. In all of these renunciations we are letting go of all of the beliefs and assumptions we have about who we are. Dimensions of deep stillness and unknowing emerge and shatter our certainties and assumptions. We travel into uncharted territories of consciousness that are the home of mystery and wonder.

Reading accounts of mystical experience we see the ways in which **profound** experiences of awakening are connected with spiritual poverty. There is cultivated in every spiritual tradition a dimension of not literal, but spiritual homelessness, which is the forerunner of discovering what it means to be at home everywhere and in all things. An ancient Zen master remarked with wonder, "When my house burned down, I gained an unobstructed view of the moonlit sky." The enduring encouragement in all great spiritual teaching is to release ourselves from all forms of ownership. Relinquishing the territorial, possessive tendencies that claim as "mine" the multiplicity of things in our inner and outer worlds, we discover a way of being where it is no longer possible to define ourselves by anything at all. Cultivating **spiritual** poverty, we release ourselves from the confinement and limitation that accompanies "me" and "mine." We discover that it is not truly possible for us to own anything at all. We come to understand that it is equally impossible to define or describe ourselves fully by any of the transient states or definitions that ripple through our hearts and minds. What remains is vastness, **stillness**, and openness.

At times, deeply ecstatic states of bliss, joy, and exultation emerge from that vastness. We encounter dimensions of silence that embrace everything that arises and passes in our world. There may be a sense of the body dissolving into light, perceptions of emptiness, visions, and energetic experiences. At times what emerges is an acute sensitivity in all of our senses, and we are profoundly moved by the simplest of sounds and sights. With a heightened **awareness** we may sense the rapidity of impermanence in all things and the very fragile nature of everything that is born. We may **rediscover** the wonder of a child, who can be delighted and fascinated by the texture and color of a single pebble on the path. We truly sense that silence is imbued with an immense energy that we had only glimpsed before.

We may rediscover the wonder of a child, who can be delighted and fascinated by the texture and color of a single pebble on the path.

Cultivating spiritual poverty, we release ourselves from the confinement and limitation that accompanies "me" and "mine."

The enduring encouragement in all great spiritual teaching is to release ourselves from all forms of ownership.

Relinquishing the territorial, possessive tendencies that claim as "mine" the multiplicity of things in our inner and outer worlds, we discover a way of being where it is no longer possible to define ourselves by anything at all.

counter dimensions of silence that embrace every

Needless to say, "unknowing" is not always a comfortable experience. It can also be a place of deep unease and anxiety. In these new realms of experience we may stumble across a feeling of existential uncertainty, as if we are standing on quicksand. We directly experience the **fleeting** nature of everything we encounter inwardly and outwardly, and feel bereft of all certainty and safety. We wonder what we can rely on, and sense the impossibility of trying to grasp the ungraspable. We face the age-old dilemma of wondering who we are apart from everything we have accumulated, gained, and **achieved**. We sense the dying away of everything we have assumed, subscribed to, and concluded, and enter into what is at times described as the "dark night of the soul." In this dark place it is worth remembering that the darkness is an essential part of our journey. The pain we experience can be thought of as growing pain—the emergence of our true selves from the chrysalis of our old selves.

Darkness is an essential part of our journey to enlightenment.

In every **spiritual** descent there will be a period of night in which there is no sure ground. In the falling away of our world as we have previously known and described it to ourselves, we may experience intense feelings of loss, despair, and even bereavement. In the **intensity** of those feelings, we are tempted to flee from ourselves and attempt to reorder and redefine reality, yet we cannot deny the truth of the understandings that have changed us. Existential anxiety is the passageway we walk down as we travel from familiar territory into the unknown. It takes

profound faith, dedication, and perseverance to remain steady, clear, and committed in the midst of these **profound** inner changes. What sustains us is our devotion to awakening, to freedom, and to realization.

Silence reveals

Silence reveals the countless births and deaths occurring in each **moment** of our lives. Sounds, sights, thoughts, sensations, and emotions appear and fade away with remarkable rapidity in the absence of holding or controlling. The inner experience of change we perceive so acutely is reflected in everything around us: love changes to anger, excitement to depression, tenderness to harshness and confidence to uncertainty. Everything that we have so carefully constructed, gained, and struggled to possess will at some point dissolve. The people we love and the people we detest are equally subject to the natural rhythms of change. We cannot hold on to anything, we cannot preserve anything. The stream of disturbing revelations threatens to overwhelm us.

Stillness acquaints us

Stillness acquaints us with reality, and it is not always a reality we welcome. As our old means of defending and protecting ourselves fall away, we may feel a sense of despondency or meaninglessness rising within us. We may wonder what the point of creating anything at all is, if time will only bear witness to its dissolution. What is the point of connection if it ends only in loss? We need all our courage to face these questions.

As we find the patience to hold these doubts as open questions, rather than conclusions, they go through their own metamorphosis. Instead of sinking into despair, we begin to experience a new appreciation for the preciousness of life and of each moment. This sunset, this laugh of a child, this taste, this feeling is **unique**, never to be repeated in exactly the same way. We find ourselves deeply treasuring the simple realities of each moment, the encounters we have with another person, and the **life** we are in. We understand that this life is to be lived fully if it is to be lived at all.

Reaching new levels of stillness or higher realms of consciousness, we may encounter the peril of spiritual ambitiousness. We are tempted to construct a new, more "spiritual" identity on the basis of some of the experiences we encounter, and find ourselves in a familiar position of fearing their loss. We forget that even the most exalted state of consciousness or transcendent feeling of bliss is also an experience that will change. In the face of change we may fall into old patterns of trying to preserve the inner growth or of setting new goals and ambitions to achieve. We can go through this cycle many times until it occurs to us that even the most profound spiritual experience is not a destination in itself but a gateway to awakening.

From the dizzying heights of bliss and communion we can easily fall back into separation and confusion many times. As we do so, we begin to learn a **profound** lesson: experiences in themselves are not so significant in the journey to enlightenment. We may attempt to grasp hold of experiences and try to add them to our "spiritual portfolios." However, we soon realize they are just passing states that do little to change our lives in themselves. What are truly significant, we come to understand, are the insights

that we can garner through the experiences. These insights fundamentally transform us and our understanding of existence. We come to understand that experiences hold within them the potential to be gateways to deep compassion and **wisdom**. We begin to look for the lessons behind our experiences.

Aversion is one of the painful and obstructive companions that can appear in the journey of awakening. As we begin to glimpse a way of being in ourselves and in the world that feels profoundly **meaningful**, we may begin to feel a subtle disdain for what we begin to label as "worldly" pursuits. We look down on a world that seems so lost in its preoccupations, busyness, and agitation, and begin to feel a kind of spiritual superiority. We may begin to find ourselves constructing a new value system, in which we separate the sacred from the mundane, the spiritual from the worldly, and the worthy from the unworthy. Soon we begin to experience the familiar tension that accompanies every **duality**. We treasure, pursue,

and cling to everything that satisfies our new, personal values and we endeavor to avoid, reject, or judge everything that we have labeled unworthy. The painfulness of duality and separation becomes increasingly evident, and we finally come to understand that this, too, is something to be let go of. Increasingly, we come to understand the wisdom of taking a position nowhere and holding onto nothing, for these are the actions that open us to be touched and taught by all things.

With dedication we learn to be at ease in not knowing. Our eyes and hearts are opened. We understand that we are on a journey, and we do not know even if it has an end. This understanding is welcomed. There may be no bottom to depth. There may always be new horizons to be probed, new possibilities to explore. Every step, every breath, and every moment is embraced as a gateway to awakening. The joy is in the beginnings we make, in our willingness to open the doors in our lives that invite us to deepen in wisdom and compassion. The greatest of all joys is to feel genuinely awake in the midst of all things.

When we dedicate ourselves to seeking a full and meaningful existence, we realize that nothing is too big, too small, too new, too old, too personal, or too objective to teach us. We are open to receive the lessons in each moment of our awareness, from the rich array of channels that wisdom flows through. We learn from the raindrop and the tear, from the snowflake and the sigh. We learn.

intimacy and solitude **both**

remind us to live a heartfelt **life** 208

Sometimes the words we hear from another person who has

emerged from experiences of great torment with a new

understanding of the human heart inspire us to reach within

ourselves to find the source of compassion and freedom.

The birth of a child, the intimacy found with a loving partner, the delight in the happiness of another, the joy of giving, and the joy of stillness are powerful gateways to awakening.

---

mystical experience is the cultivation of wonder

Great mystics and teachers emerge from the seclusion of their monasteries and cells to speak of the radical transformations they have encountered. Just as the paths to awakening are many and varied, so too are the accounts of what it means to awaken. As we delve into the rich spiritual literature that is the legacy of the realized, it is as if we are listening to the different instruments that

make up an orchestra. All of them have their unique, wondrous sound, yet they meet in playing the same symphony. Some of these mystics have consciously cultivated a spiritual discipline over years that has led to a profound upheaval in their consciousness and way of engaging in life. For others, their meeting with the spirit seems almost accidental. Profound spiritual openings are at times born within very ordinary encounters that are seen with new eyes. The message that is consistently conveyed in all the stories of awakening is a message of profound joy and freedom. It is a message that cannot be wholly expressed in words and that can be truly understood only through personal experience.

Spiritual pilgrims throughout time speak of "waking up from a dream," communion with the divine, discovering their true nature, or being absorbed into the wonder of oneness. The language of the mystics reflects the cultural and religious flavor of their life. Christian mystics describe being filled with the Holy Spirit; Hindus speak of the discovery of their "true self."

In the Zen tradition students are encouraged to discover the "face they wore before they were born"; and in other Buddhist traditions the spiritual journey is described as a path to "Nirvana." Mystics do not argue with one another. Beneath the multiplicity of descriptions, spiritual journeys share a celebration of wisdom, freedom, and a profound understanding of the sacred.

Mystical experience is the cultivation of wonder. The German poet Rainer Maria Rilke wrote, "Existence can still enchant us; in a hundred places we find it wells and springs. A play of pure forces that no one can touch without wanting to kneel in **wonder**." Spiritual awakening is not primarily concerned with grand and exotic once-in-a-lifetime experiences, but in discovering a way of being in which we celebrate the startling miracles found in our everyday **realities**. To be truly awake is to forsake habitual numbness, to live fully the moments so easily lost in habit, to cultivate the willingness to be surprised, and to discover an unshakable wisdom. There are new beginnings in each moment of our life. The rapture of simply being alive emerges from the awakened heart.

The awakening of our hearts and minds is mysterious and unpredictable. Spiritual awakening is not the sole territory of the cloistered saints and mystics. The spiritual openings that truly awaken us often come unexpected and unannounced. Countless people in our world have experienced moments of genuine spiritual awakening, in which their perception of reality shifts and they open to a new way of seeing and understanding. Our perception and understanding are frequently radically altered by the events of our lives, just as changes in our consciousness deeply alter how we see the events we encounter. Awakening, it seems, is not always the result of years of heroic, grueling effort and training. Awakening comes when our hearts are open and still, when we are willing to suspend our busyness and step beyond the boundaries of fear.

Our life is a journey of awakening:

it requires us only to be still, receptive, and present. The events of our lives continue to have the power to startle us into new ways of seeing and deeper understandings of reality. It is futile to seek awakening outside of ourselves or apart from this life. Everything we need for profound understanding and deep compassion is offered to us in the events and encounters of each moment. The path of awakening is simply cultivating our capacity to be deeply touched and moved by the life and world we are part of. What is found on the mountaintops and in the deserts that the mystics retreat to is the same world found in our cities and ordinary

lives. What is cultivated by the mystics on their mountaintops and deserts is a deep dedication to stillness and to listening deeply. It is this dedication we are invited to nurture in each moment of our lives—we should not think that there is a proper setting for awakening.

One of the timeless stories of a

journey of awakening is found within the Buddha's quest for enlightenment. The young, cosseted Prince Siddhartha left the comfort and security of his palace to explore the delights of the world. What he encountered instead in the streets of the city was the sight of an elderly woman, a sickly man, a corpse, and a wandering renunciate. These simple sights had the power to startle Siddhartha, to challenge his assumptions, and to radically alter his previously held views of reality. It was the beginning of his quest to discover a deeper sense of meaning, an enduring peace, and an understanding of what it means to be free. Siddhartha left his life of ease to journey into the unknown.

None of us is so protected in our life that we can ignore the reality that we live in a fragile world and body. We all meet the reality of aging, death, and uncertainty on a daily basis. When we are lost in numbness we endeavor heroically to exclude the implications of these realities from our consciousness. When we are still and receptive we are touched and moved by reality. We find ourselves seeking to understand what it means to be free, to live a compassionate and meaningful life, and to nurture within ourselves a quality of consciousness that is not governed by the changing circumstances and events of life. We come to understand that the **freedom** we seek will not be born of rejecting our life or world but of greeting it as a teacher, a "heavenly messenger" that reminds us of our own capacity to discover a limitless, immeasurable freedom. Awakening is not always predictable or linear, nor a state we can possess. We may imagine that awakening will come to us only through grand spiritual experience and breakthrough. We may project freedom into a future time. It

is deeply important to understand that awakening is **immanent**. The great mystics of the past and present consistently remind us to discover the freedom and mystery of this moment. The eternal message is to open our eyes and hearts, to still our minds and discover the freedom and wakefulness available to us in this moment.

Joy and sorrow are both powerful catalysts of awakening. At times we discover that joy and sorrow are found in the same event and place. A young woman spoke of her experience of being hit by a motorcycle. In the moments between the time she was struck and sent flying and the time she finally hit the ground she experienced a dimension of consciousness of pure **stillness**, timelessness, and vastness. Later, while she was lying in the emergency room of the hospital, the doctors mistook her joy and laughter for symptoms of concussion. Those few moments changed her life, revealing to her a dimension of reality that was limitless, free, and truly **awake**. It was the beginning of a profound spiritual quest.

An elderly woman entered a hospice, filled with a deep bitterness, resentment, and anger that poisoned her every moment. It was the same bitterness she had carried through her life, that had served to alienate her from her children and her friends, and left her alone and isolated. One night as she lay in bed, enduring the pain of her body and the torture of her embittered mind, she spoke of a shift that seemed to happen in the very foundations of her heart. Her heart opened as she understood the way in which the pain she was going through was the pain being experienced by countless women in the universe in that moment. She felt the pain of the ailing migrant worker, the helplessness of low-caste Indian women sentenced to a lifetime of drudgery, and the despair of the abandoned children in the slums of Rio. As her heart opened she began to understand that she was not a victim of life but of her own resentment and anger. A deep peace spread through her heart, and even the agony of her body began to ease. In the morning the nurses, usually reluctant to enter her room, were stunned to be met with kindness and sensitivity.

A young man in the midst of a meditation retreat found himself sitting with an aching back, a restless mind, and a persistent wish to be anywhere but where he was. He opened his eyes to see his fellow students sitting with apparent calm and could feel only envy of and antipathy to them. As he struggled with the torment of his mind and body, it suddenly came to him that there was in truth nowhere for him to go and nowhere to hide. He remembered the endless cycles he had gone through in his life of avoidance, resistance, and rejection. To his amazement he found himself softening, turning toward the pain he was experiencing. His aches began to fade, and a startling sense of lightness and transparency began to saturate his body. The churning thoughts began to disappear, and he was absorbed into an experience of light and peace.

From early adolescence, a young woman trained hard to be a professional runner and dreamed of a future filled with the triumphs and awards that her skill would bring. When she was sixteen she began to experience numbness in parts of her body, times when she would stumble unpredictably, and sometimes a debilitating physical fatigue. For a time, she tried to ignore what was happening to her and to continue with her training as if nothing was wrong. Inevitably her symptoms worsened, and she was finally diagnosed with motoneuron disease. For weeks she spiraled down into deep depression and despair. One morning as she lay in bed with tears rolling down her cheeks, she turned her head and was struck by the multitude of flowers and cards that filled her bedroom. She spoke of how she suddenly realized the depth and abundance of love and care that surrounded her. In that moment, her heart broke in a new way as she understood how she was embraced in the hearts of so many people.

217

All of us encounter moments of sorrow, loss, disappointment, and separation that grieve us deeply. Our worlds are shattered, and we open to a world that seems to have changed in a moment. These are all events that hold the potential to be moments of genuine awakening. We can revert to familiar pathways of blame, despair, or numbness, or we can open to the teaching and wonder of these moments. They invite us to see in a new way, to feel more deeply, and to discover a genuine sense of inner freedom.

We can revert to familiar

pathways of blame,

despair, or numbness, or

we can open to the

teaching and wonder of

these moments. They invite

us to see in a new way, to

feel more deeply, and to

discover a genuine sense

of inner freedom.

Endings invite us to learn, not to shrink

Joy is often extraordinarily simple.

Joy, too, can be a powerful instigator of transformation. The birth of a child, the intimacy found with a loving partner, the delight in the happiness of another, the joy of giving, and the joy of stillness are powerful gateways to awakening. At times in our lives we need to reach out and touch joy, to connect with what it is in this life that makes our hearts sing. Do we take the moments to watch the setting sun, to listen to the robin outside our window, and to embrace the grandeur of a majestic tree? Do we take the moments to watch a bud unfolding, to celebrate the first faltering steps of an infant, or to listen wholeheartedly to the sounds of the wind in the trees? Do we take the time to seek spiritual sustenance, to nurture the seeds of sensitivity and compassion within us? Joy is not always so distant or elusive—it may be as close to us as our own breath. Joy awakens us to the possibility of a deep, heartfelt happiness that is both ordinary and mystical. Joy is often extraordinarily simple. A great teacher once remarked upon the profound joy discovered in not being anyone, not going anywhere, and not wanting anything. Joy is most often found in our capacity to be wholeheartedly present and open to life, to wonder at its mystery, and to be moved by all of its textures.

Silence reveals a profound joy. The Buddha once taught that the path of awakening is the path of happiness that leads to the highest happiness, and the highest happiness is peace. Spiritual awakening is the discovery of joy; the joy of being awake and the joy of freedom. The gateways to the spirit are many. Sometimes the words of another person, who has emerged from experiences of great torment with a new understanding of the human heart, inspire us to reach within ourselves to find compassion and freedom. People continue to emerge from concentration camps, prisons, deprivation, and experiences of genocide with their hearts deepened, their capacity to forgive ripened, and with remarkable inner freedom.

ssible for all of us to live in a sacred way. The intentions we bring to how we live our lives are what transforms the

It is possible for all of us to live in a **sacred** way. The intentions we bring to how we live our lives are what transforms them. Nurturing within us the willingness to probe beneath the surface of things, to let go, and to live with a **wise** and compassionate heart creates a sacred space in each moment of our life. With the intention to see deeply and to learn from the simple realities of our lives, we begin to understand what it means to live with a **meditative** spirit.

Enlightenment is the path to the end of sorrow,

fear, and alienation. It is the source of

immeasurable joy, creativity, and peace.

Enlightenment is more than a transient experience.

Enlightenment does not divorce us from the world but teaches us to engage in this world with the compassion and care it so desperately needs.

ENLIGHTENMENT

one who knows eternity is called enlightened

Over the centuries men and women have retreated to the cloisters and deserts, remaining secluded and still for months or years. Others follow a different discipline, living a life of dedicated service and selflessness, caring for the impoverished, the imprisoned, and the disenfranchised. Whether they adopt an intensive inner spiritual discipline or an arduous path of giving, they are heeding the same call. The possibility of enlightenment and the call to awaken continue to be powerful longings. Many of these same men and women have emerged from seclusion bearing a visible grace, a powerful stillness, and a boundless compassion. We feel impelled to question what the Buddha understood when he sat under the Bodhi Tree on the eve of his enlightenment. What was revealed to Teresa of Avila and Julian of Norwich within the walls of their cloisters? What is it that enables the Dalai Lama to forgive and live with a powerful compassion and generosity? What was the source of Gandhi's inner dedication, which enabled him to persevere in his search for **freedom** against the powerful obstacles he faced?

When we listen closely to the words and teachings of the great mystics and spiritual teachers who have traveled the path before us, we come to understand that what they have undertaken is a profound spiritual **transformation**. We hear the message of liberation, of enlightenment, in their poetry, in their stories, and sometimes through the radiance of their smiles.

Beneath the tomes of literature, the variety of techniques, and the differing spiritual vocabularies we sense the central **mystery** that lies at the heart of every spiritual tradition. It is the mystery of revelation, of the timeless and limitless. It is the knowing of the unknowable, the mystery of the divine, **liberation**, and a sacred oneness. It is impossible to portray this great mystery adequately in words—at times it is simply called "enlightenment." In the *Tao Te Ching* it is said, "Going back to the origin is called peace; it means reversion to destiny. Reversion to destiny is called **eternity**. One who knows eternity is called enlightened."

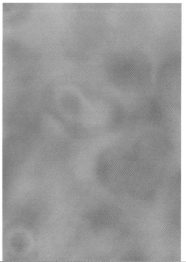

we sense the mystery that lies at the heart of every spiritual tradition

We already are everything that we are seeking.

Awakening can be truly understood only through direct experience—through stillness, opening, and deepening. This is our journey.

If enlightenment is truly timeless and limitless it will be found in the flowers and the stones, the rivers and the clouds, in this body, and in all bodies, in this mind and in all minds. We must simply learn to see.

We come to understand that our spiritual journey is not to emulate the saints and mystics of the past or present, but to understand what they have understood.

When we are floundering in the storms of confusion, obsession, and restlessness we may regard the stories of awakening written by half-starved mystics huddled in caves with skepticism or even cynicism, imagining them to be the **hallucinations** of the deranged or the propaganda of the religious.

As we begin to discover a greater inner stillness and to attend to our own spirit, the poetry of enlightenment echoes more and more deeply in our own hearts. We come to understand that our spiritual **journey** is not to emulate the saints and mystics of the past or present, but to understand what they have understood. Their stories are like fingers pointing at the moon, not to be mistaken for the moon itself, but simply showing us the way.

The sacred stories **inspire** us, enliven us, and awaken us to the possibilities of silence, yet we cannot learn from them about enlightenment. Awakening can be truly understood only through direct experience—through stillness, opening, and deepening. This is our journey.

The poetry and stories of enlightenment attempt to communicate the unexplainable, to give form to the formless. Reading these stories we are inclined to form images of what enlightenment is and to try to find experiences that conform to our images. It is a frustrating and futile task. As we learn to listen to the teachings of the realized with greater and greater **stillness** we come to understand that enlightenment is the shattering of all of our pictures and images. We cannot make ourselves enlightened; our journey may be one of gradual learning to remove the veils of confusion that obstruct awakening. Ancient masters remind us not to seek liberation and enlightenment outside of ourselves but to open our eyes and see that all things are the very essence of **liberation**. We already are everything that we are seeking. If enlightenment is truly timeless and limitless it will be found in the flowers and the stones, the rivers and the clouds, in this body and in all bodies, in this mind and in all minds. We must simply learn to see.

Every great spiritual path is dedicated to awakening and holds at its heart the possibility of enlightenment. Liberation is our spiritual destiny. Sacred poetry describes enlightenment as timeless grace, immeasurable consciousness, divine oneness, and limitless freedom. Mystics struggle with words to describe the indescribable, to make known the unknowable. Yet their words communicate a profound richness, joy, and liberation. Mystics do not tell the same story, nor do they describe the same path to travel. They share in conveying an ineffable joy and freedom. They speak about the end of struggle and sorrow, the dissolution of separation and division, and the awakening to vastness.

Followers of many different religion sects hold tales of enlightenment.

There is an obvious, collective humility that permeates all the accounts of awakening. Enlightenment is not a personal possession or achievement. The boundaries of the personal have dissolved in the face of awakening. What is frequently recounted is the "nothing special" nature of enlightenment. The Buddha recounted, "I gained absolutely nothing from complete, unexcelled enlightenment. This is why it is complete, unexcelled enlightenment." Awakening, it seems, does not make us "holy," "perfect," or "saintly." These are the goals of the unawakened, confined within the boundaries of a separate "self." Enlightenment, it seems, does not make us "anyone" at all, and this is the essence of freedom. The saintly person clearly carries no notions of what it means to be "good" or "saintly." The enlightened person sees nothing but the divine in the presence of all things. The truly compassionate person has no notion of "saving" others. Yet an awakened life is naturally expressed in compassion, service, and joy. An ancient Zen saying reminds us, "Before enlightenment I chopped wood and carried water. After enlightenment I chopped wood and carried water."

Dame Julian of Norwich

(c.1372–c.1418) was one of the earliest Christian women to write of their encounters with God. She writes about seeing her soul "so large as it were an endless world, and also as it were a blessed kingdom and understood that it is a worshipful city." She spoke of the limitlessness of God's

love, manifested in all things, embracing all things, and the essence of all things. She saw God's love as "warm clothing that wraps and enfolds us" and the love that dissolved all separations. "In love" she says, "we have our beginning" and "love is without beginning."

A contemporary mystic has spoken of what he remembers as the best day in his life, when, inexplicably, he simply stopped thinking. "Walking in the garden words suddenly failed me. All the mental chatter and imagination for no apparent reason died down. Past and future dropped away and suddenly I was embraced in something I can only call 'silence.' It was if I had been born anew in that moment, with no name, no history, and no future. The sound of the bird was heard in my heart, the warmth of the sun touched my skeleton. It was as if all ideas of 'inner' and 'outer' were suddenly absurd. All I sensed was a vast emptiness that had room for everything. I felt like I had lost myself but gained eternity."

Mystics, as well as "ordinary" people, from the past and present have tried to describe the experience of meeting a higher level of consciousness and being. A great teacher of the past speaks of what he can describe only as a "collision with the unfathomable." He relates that while he was sitting in meditation, "spontaneously there was a sudden eruption that shattered my poise and sense of order. My body seemed to disappear and my consciousness expanded into space. A vast stillness and joy arose that asked for no explanation. I opened my eyes and saw out the window the trees and hills I had gazed at a thousand times before, but it was if I had never seen them before. I felt embraced in something I can only call 'isness' but in truth there is no word that can describe the ineffable peace of that moment. It was as if I saw infinity. I do not know how long this lasted but when I emerged from my room in the evening I understood that something had changed forever. I left something behind in that moment. I think I would call it struggle."

A young woman spoke of volunteering to work in a village hospital in India. "A lot of my time I spent judging. Many of the illnesses were just a result of ignorance. I resented the poverty, I resented the rich, I resented people who lived indifferent to the daily grind of so many of these villagers. I blamed people for having borne all the children they couldn't care for and I blamed myself for blaming everyone. I was a knot of tension. One of my jobs was to tend to the ulcers that formed on the bodies of the malnourished children. One boy had to come for treatment over many days. First he would cry and struggle, but then seemed to descend into a resignation too old for his years. As I held him on my lap one day and looked into his eyes I felt something shift within me. It was as if I was holding myself as an infant, helpless, innocent and in pain. I seemed to lose myself in his eyes and it became so utterly obvious that I did not exist in the way I thought I did. There was a great relief in this, a surrender, a giving way and a freedom I had never conceived of."

Within stillness there lies the possibility of profound transformation. We are changed, our understanding of reality is transformed.

A young Westerner undergoing a long and arduous meditation retreat spoke of stepping into a timeless, inner space. "As my body and mind calmed, it was not as if the world disappeared but everything was suddenly remarkably transparent. Nothing held any solidity, nor was there any difference between here and there, far and near. It was obviously ridiculous to try to explain the world or myself. It felt like I'd suddenly woken up from a deep sleep. In everything there shone the unutterable, unshakable joy of reality. Beginnings and endings, 'you' and 'me,' 'inner' and 'outer,' suddenly made no sense. There arose a profound sense of release, yet I couldn't even describe what is was I was released from."

Within stillness there lies the possibility of profound transformation. We are changed, our understanding of reality is transformed. Contemporary and ancient mystics speak of the release and freedom of awakening. Liberation, it seems, is not about improving ourselves or getting rid of anything, but is concerned with a deeper understanding of this very life. Enlightenment is the path to the end of sorrow, fear, and alienation. It is the source of immeasurable joy, creativity, and peace. Enlightenment is more than a transient experience, although deep experiences of awakening reveal to us a way of seeing and being we had never before imagined. The essence of enlightenment is a profound transformation in our consciousness that forever changes us.

Liberation is not a solution to the sorrows and challenges of living. Enlightenment is not a magical panacea that cures and eradicates the demands or hardships that life will continue to present to us. Liberation is not a defense against life but teaches us to engage our lives with a deep serenity and wisdom. We cannot prevent some of the pain and change that will occur in our bodies as we age. Loss brings with it sorrow; death brings grief; separation brings heartache—enlightenment is not a

It is our capacity to feel deeply that connects us with the human community, bringing empathy and compassion.

Deep liberating insight can release us from the world of anxiety, discontent and struggle. Liberating understanding releases us from the turmoil of confusion, attachment, and alienation. Liberation releases us to live fully, to be wholeheartedly present in all the moments of our lives, and to live with the true nature of all things. Enlightenment teaches us what it means to be free, to forsake all sense of confinement, and to live within a timeless peace.

cessation of feeling. It is our capacity to feel deeply that connects us with the human community, bringing empathy and compassion. Deep, liberating insight can release us from the world of anxiety, discontent, and struggle. Liberating understanding releases us from the turmoil of confusion, attachment, and alienation. Liberation releases us to live fully, to be wholeheartedly present in all the moments of our lives, and to live in harmony with the true nature of all things. Enlightenment teaches us what it means to be free, to forsake all sense of confinement, and to live within a timeless peace.

The freedom born of profound understanding is radically different from our conventional notions of freedom. Culturally, we live with an illusion of freedom. We believe we are free to pursue our desires, to say what we want, and sometimes to act without regard for the consequences of our actions. We cherish the freedom to proclaim territorial rights on possessions and even

people, and resent the intrusion of anything that hinders what we call our "personal" freedom. When we examine this sense of freedom closely we see it to be extraordinarily dependent and fragile. How free do we feel when our desires are frustrated, our ambitions hindered, or our expectations disappointed? Genuine freedom is neither a permission nor an entitlement. It is the inner vastness that cannot be confined by anything, that is not dependent on anyone or anything, and that is deeply rooted in integrity, wisdom, and compassion. It is freedom from self-inflicted suffering, anguish, turmoil, and discontent. It is the freedom from attachment, self-centeredness, and clinging that releases genuine, limitless joy. It is the freedom from the subtle and obvious habits of our lives and hearts that enables us to be truly awake and present in our lives.

We begin to see how futile it is to look for genuine freedom in any external source. Silence asks us to rethink our understanding of freedom and to look for it within ourselves and in our relationship with the world.

An enlightened heart is a creative heart, responsive and engaged with the world. Enlightenment does not divorce us from the world but teaches us to engage in this world with the compassion and care it so desperately needs.

Enlightenment reveals the possibility of peace, joy, and serenity immanent in all beings. The great enlightened sages and teachers of the past and present do not hoard their wisdom in secret but reenter the world with a profound commitment to bring about the end of suffering, alienation, and distress wherever they encounter it. Wisdom and compassion are likened to the two wings of a bird. Profound wisdom finds its expression in deep compassion; without this expression it has little meaning. We seek awakening not to serve ourselves, but to serve others. In serving others, we understand, we serve, and care for ourselves in the deepest way possible.

The freedom of awakening is found in the cessation of discontent, alienation, and turmoil. It is found within our own hearts, minds, and lives. Discovering the richness of stillness we simultaneously find ourselves increasingly awake in our lives. We learn to attend with compassion to those places in our minds and hearts where we are lost, stuck, driven, or confused. We learn to cultivate the understanding that releases us from the confinement of our obsessions, compulsions, and agitation. Awakening, we discover, may not be so far away. It awaits our discovery in each moment of our lives. Enlightenment is not just a historical story. It is a possibility for each of us, born of the dedication we bring to stillness, understanding, and awakening.

an awakened life is a **compassionate** and conscious **life**
240

Relying less on acquisition and possession to provide us with gratification, we discover the happiness and peace born of having less, wanting less, and needing less.

We can never gain enough to soothe a discontented heart. We can discover a profound sanctuary of peace and richness in simplicity and stillness.

silence is the home of awareness

Enlightenment is not the end of the spiritual story. The wealth of sacred literature tends to emphasize the solitary pilgrimages of the wise and awakened sages who inspire us to follow in their footsteps. We are heartened by their stories of spiritual breakthroughs and discoveries, but we need to read on. We revere these people not for their enlightened experiences, but for

the impact they have upon the world we live in. The accounts of great spiritual journeys follow a familiar rhythm of seclusion, transformation, and emergence. We leave the marketplace only to return; we retreat from the haste and busyness of our world and return to find it unchanged. What does change is our way of seeing and being in the marketplace and busyness of our world.

Every mystic emerging from the cloisters or descending from the mountaintop will be tested by their journey back into the world. Their return is not always greeted with applause; their understandings may meet indifference, and they find themselves faced with the challenge of embodying their **wisdom** Spiritual journeys are radical and often countercultural. Mystics are

We return to our everyday lives from the heights of silence, transformed and enlightened.

at heart revolutionaries and dissidents. The British Raj did not welcome Gandhi's call for freedom. The social and cultural structures of the Deep South were deeply reluctant to embrace the equality and dignity called for by Martin Luther King, Jr.. The early women mystics in the Christian tradition were often reviled for their understanding of God as love rather than wrathful and punitive. The Buddha and Christ were both revolutionaries, overturning cultural and religious assumptions and beliefs. We rarely turn on our televisions and hear that today is a good day to "let go" and to cultivate compassion. An integral part of every awakening is understanding what is true, living fearlessly in the spirit of truth, and embodying our understanding in every area of our lives. Enlightenment is the dawn of a new way of being in the world.

Genuine understanding can be lived only here and now, embodied in every detail of our lives. None of us are sustained or nourished by memories of past experience, no matter how wonderful or enlightening. Neither can we find sustenance in visions of the future. We are nourished by the dedication to living our understanding in this moment and nurturing the compassion, integrity, and wisdom that are the source of all peace and joy. Life will continue to ask us to "let go;" our adversaries will continue to invite us to find new depths of tolerance and generosity, and the changing events and losses in our lives will always remind us of the need to find stillness and balance within our own hearts. Our lives are the path we walk, and awakening is the beginning of a path and a life of freedom.

We can all learn to be present, awake, and open to the possibility of genuine compassion and balance in our lives.

Awakening is not an accident. The variety of paths and traditions of spiritual descent cannot guarantee awakening or **liberation**. They show to us a way of cultivating an inner climate of heart and mind that is receptive to deep understanding and profound transformation. Those who have traveled the path of awakening before us have started in exactly the same place that we begin and have been asked to learn the same lessons that we are invited to learn.

In the midst of our lives we can learn to nurture an inner environment of calm and sensitivity that is susceptible to transformation. We can all learn to bring a greater stillness into our lives as we surrender the **illusion** that busyness is the same as meaningfulness and that productivity is the same as true richness. We can all learn to be present, awake, and open to the possibility of genuine compassion and balance in our lives. As we hold ourselves ready to act with compassion, it gradually becomes our natural resting stance, rather than a result of great effort.

A spiritual journey is essentially a way of being deeply honest with ourselves. In the quest for awakening we undertake a careful examination of our lives, seeing where we are awake and where we live in the thrall of habit. We learn to see where we are a **captive** of attachment, confusion, and turmoil. Listening inwardly, we discover the old resentments and disappointments that linger in our **hearts**. Examining our lives, we come to learn the ways in which we consciously or unconsciously travel the pathways of confusion through distractedness and **fantasy**, and the various ways we disconnect ourselves from the moment. Spiritual honesty is not wrathful or harsh; there is little wisdom in instituting a more enlightened, spiritual censor into our lives. Wise honesty is not concerned with judgment, rebuke, or greater self-consciousness but with the ending of sorrow and turmoil. No one outside of ourselves, no matter how loving or wise, can truly understand the dynamics of our own hearts or liberate us from the confusion that swirls within us.

Many of our habits of confusion and agitation have a long history; this does not imply that they must have an equally long future. In countless ways and moments we can all learn to be **still** and calm, to listen more deeply, and to bring to a close our familiar, habitual patterns of disconnection and restlessness. We learn to bring a kind **attention** to the darkest and most habitual places in our lives, simply because they are places of pain.

Habit comes to an end in just one moment of wholehearted attention. Instead of answering the telephone with impatience, traveling to work with only our arrival in mind, filling the gaps in our day with fantasy, or devouring our meals mindlessly, we can learn to approach all of these moments as moments of possibility. What does it feel like to truly pay attention, to be wholeheartedly present and sensitive? The simplest moments in our day are transformed into magical moments of connection simply because we are alive within them. This new way of being needs regular maintenance for it to be fully present in our lives.

A path of awakening is living in a way that inclines us to be receptive to awakening rather than susceptible to confusion. Spiritual **honesty** is embodied in the integrity we bring to all of the interactions in our lives. Communication that springs from anger, fear, or need serves always to foster alienation and the heavy burden of regret, guilt, and anxiety that it leaves in our minds. Words that are spoken with mindfulness, care, and sensitivity are powerful communicators of kindness and compassion, leaving no residue of alienation behind them. Integrity is cultivated in the choices we make in our lives and in the actions we engage in or leave undone. Integrity leaves behind it a climate of calm stillness in our hearts; it is a forsaking of confusion and agitation.

We do not have to stop the world to be still within ourselves. We do need to bring wholehearted attention and a commitment to being present in order to discover stillness. Throughout our days we can remember to

feel the touch of our feet on the ground, to listen fully to the person who is speaking to us, to feel our breath moving in our bodies, and to **attend** to what is right in front of us. We can carry stillness with us into the business of our day. We can always, no matter where we are, what we are doing, or whom we are with, remind ourselves of the happiness of just being and the joy of stillness.

Sitting in an Asian monastery that was undergoing yet another phase of construction work, a young student complained to the abbot, "How can I meditate with all this noise?" The abbot answered, "How can you not?"

Silence changes us. We learn to

live in a more respectful relationship to our inner and outer worlds. In doing this, we acknowledge our own and other people's value and worth. We do not choose to judge or condemn—either ourselves or anyone else. We simply strive to live an honest and open life, aiming to bring an end to suffering and pain as we come across it. We also cultivate a more respectful relationship to our bodies and to all bodies. An embodied spirituality begins by learning to bring compassion and care to our own bodies. Instead of fearing and resisting the changes our bodies inevitably go through as we age or become ill, we find ourselves humbled and compassionate. Within our relationship to our own bodies we learn to embrace the imperfect and the changing and we learn the simple but profound art of living in **harmony** with what is.

Within our bodies we see reflected the life and journey of all bodies. We see the way in which we inflict suffering upon our bodies through clinging to ideals of perfection, through resisting change, and through judgment. We learn a new way of being present within this body and with all bodies. By the simple and heartfelt decision to live respectfully of ourselves and others, we start to truly embody the understanding we have received through silence. Sensitivity, acceptance, and generosity are the gifts of the awakened heart.

248   Sensitivity, acceptance, and generosity are the gifts of the awakened heart.

Awakening teaches us the nature of our essential interdependence and interconnectedness with all life. Understanding the profound implications of our interdependence, we see the shallowness and fear of living in a self-cherishing way. Empathy and the ethics of compassion are born of the awakened heart. Genuine inner freedom is obstructed not by the forms and events of our lives but through being lost in self-centeredness, confusion, greed, and anger. Inner freedom is revealed through our willingness to release these forces, through cultivating stillness, sensitivity, awareness, and compassion. The institutions of sorrow and pain that deny inner freedom pervade our economic, political, and military edifices. The effects of these institutions in our communities, societies, and world are injustice, inequality, deprivation, and fear. The surrender of freedom is the inevitable consequence of territorialism, possessiveness, fear, and anger. Awakening is not ethically neutral. It seeks to bring about the end of all pain, fear, and disconnection.

We often feel powerless and impotent to change the tides of violence, war, greed, and exploitation that sweep through our world. Yet we all have the capacity to be a conscious participant in creating and shaping the quality of the world we live in. Awareness reveals the illusion of helplessness. We are helpless only so long as we are lost in ideals, our fantasies of how life "should" be, and our judgments about how life is. We cease to be helpless the moment we begin to live in an awakened way. How do we care for and relate to our own communities, our environment, the person beside us, our families, and the ways we engage with our world on a moment-to-moment level? Too often, we underestimate the power of compassion and empathy. In northern Thailand the monks and nuns witnessed the devastation of ancient forests by powerful logging consortiums. Their response was to wrap the orange robes of a monk around the trunks of the trees, ordaining them as abbots. Those were the trees that survived.

Awakening is the beginning of a **creative** and a profoundly engaged life. We concern ourselves deeply with the transformations that are possible in the moment. Can we offer **forgiveness** to the people who have hurt us? We can turn our attention to the rifts and divisions that shadow our own relationships and then commit ourselves to the task of healing wounds, rather than **perpetuating** separation and conflict. Can we bring calmness and peace to the places and circumstances in our lives that are most fragmented and confused? We can explore what it means to step out of the collective agitation of our world and the impact we can have on the world around us. Can we acknowledge, with an open heart, the endless images and situations of violence, harm, and terror that life delivers to us? We can learn to forsake avoidance, resistance, and **judgment**, and cease, in our own lives, to be a cause of harm or negative impact.

The ethics of awakening teach us the joy of generosity. We can all learn to be increasingly generous with our time and attention and the quality of **presence** we bring to all of the people who come into our world. We can learn to be more tolerant and accepting. We do not need to love everyone or condone the harmful. We can stay connected and make an inner commitment not to banish anyone from our hearts. We can explore what it means to live a simpler life. Silence is the garden of **happiness** and inner abundance. Relying less upon acquisition and possession to provide us with gratification, we discover the happiness and peace born of having less, wanting less, and needing less. We can never gain enough to soothe a discontented heart. We can discover a profound sanctuary of **peace** and richness in simplicity and stillness.

Awakening grants us a newfound poise and balance, which we can take into all the events of our life.

An awakened life is a compassionate and conscious life. Silence is the home of awareness and wisdom that transforms every dimension of our lives. In silence we weep for the sorrow in our world. In silence we learn what makes our hearts sing. In silence we discover a profound understanding of inner completeness.

In silence we learn what it means to be free.

index

acknowledgments

Every effort has been made to credit the copyright holders. We apologize for any unintentional omissions. We would be pleased to insert appropriate acknowledgment in any subsequent edition of this publication.

Corbis Images 26, 138–139

Science Photo Library 42 (Henny Allis)

Siân Keogh 3 (from L to R No.3), 3 (from L to R No.5), 4 (from L to R No.6), 20, 23, 25, 27, 65, 66, 67, 109, 113, 188, 255 (from L to R No.3)

Simon Punter 92, 93, 98, 99, 102, 114, 122, 123, 124–125, 126, 130–131(t), 131(b), 133, 145, 150–151, 154, 155, 156, 158–159, 162, 168, 169, 174–175, 178, 186(b), 186–187, 227, 254 (from L to R No.3), 255 (from L to R No.4)

Steve Gorton 2 (from L to R No.1), 21, 28, 50, 51, 53, 54, 63, 68–69, 72, 75, 77, 78, 80–81, 88, 89, 91, 103, 105, 107, 108, 117, 180–181, 182, 217, 230, 231, 240, 255 (from L to R No.2)

Powerstock Zefa 19, 31, 41, 44, 45, 59, 61, 62, 73, 83, 85, 86, 104, 111, 160, 173, 179, 184, 198, 203, 206–207, 208, 224, 254 (from L to R No.1), 254 (from L to R No. 5), 255 (from L to R No.1), 255 (from L to R No.5)

Excerpt from "Keeping Quiet" from EXTRAVAGARIA by Pablo Neruda. Translated by Alastair Reid. Translation copyright 1974 by Alastair Reid. Reprinted by permission Farrar, Straus and Giroux, LLC.

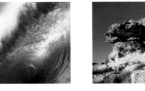